Einstein Blogging

Top Secrets to Help You Blog Smarter, Not Harder

By Forrest Webber and Megan Malone

Table of Contents

Acknowledgments

We want to thank so many people for their help with this book. Thank you to our friends and family who have supported us throughout our own blogging journeys. And thank you to the entire team at Wander Media who we have the privilege of working with every day.

Finally, we could not have created this book without the inspiration from so many successful bloggers.

Thank you to those who helped and inspired us:
> Ben Huber (DollarSprout.com)
> Susan Storm (PsychologyJunkie.com)
> Tracie Fobes (TracieFobes.com)

And a special thanks to these blogging and business heroes who have also inspired the book:
> Alex Nerney and Lauren McManus (CreateAndGo.com)
> Brian Halligan and Dharmesh Shah (HubSpot.com)
> Chris Guillebeau (ChrisGuillebeau.com)
> Darren Rowse (ProBlogger.com)
> Richard Patey (RichardPatey.com)

Introduction

I've always wanted to open a book with an outright, bold-faced lie. Here goes nothing.

The very first blogger, Ralph Waldo Emerson, famously penned, "The creation of a thousand forests is in one acorn."

The truth: Ralph *did* say those words. But he wasn't a blogger because the kind of technology we have today wasn't around back then. But if it had been, you can bet your ass he would have been a blogger.

What I'm really trying to say is this: *Starting a blog is like planting an acorn.*

Would you believe me if I told you that one of our websites has a single blog post that has earned more than $20,000? That's right—*one blog post* has been consistently creating between $1,000 and $2,500 per month of revenue for more than two years.

Moreover, this blog post spawned a series of additional blog post ideas, which now generate revenue of their own. Do you see the acorn compounding into a forest?

There's more.

What makes an acorn grow? With the proper soil (mindset), nurturing (consistent effort), and sunlight (market factors), you can create something much bigger than you have ever imagined. Something that provides a harvest for people around the world. And while the harvest is for everyone, *you get to sell the crops.*

That's a big deal because it tugs at two of the biggest heartstrings of nearly every human: the desire for independence and the longing for purpose.

What feels better than providing a bountiful harvest that makes others happy *and* reaping tremendous monetary rewards that make *you* happy?

These desires aren't in competition. And when brought into alignment, these desires operate like two cylinders of an engine, fueling you to create a bright future for yourself and others.

The acorn is your blog—and it's planting season.

— *Forrest*

CHAPTER 1

Getting Started

The alarm on your nightstand slowly wakes you up from a deep slumber. You were sailing on a boat, somewhere in the North Atlantic. In your old life, waking from such a peaceful dream would be a drag but not now.

You touch your bare feet to the cool ground beneath your bed and take a deep breath. You walk to the window and draw the curtains. Then you turn on your morning playlist as you dance into the kitchen to start a pot of coffee.

It's a Wednesday, and you have a full work schedule ahead. But it could be any day of the week. Because today, just like every other day, you get to do something you love.

If you've been blogging for a while, you understand the freedom that comes from being a blogging entrepreneur. If you're just getting started, the scenario above may sound as foreign as a long-lost folk tale.

Regardless of where you are on your journey, this book will help you learn how to create a sustainable, purpose-driven business without sacrificing the freedom and fulfillment you started your blog to find in the first place.

Who is this book for?

This book is for purpose-seekers, adventurers, and searchers of mystery and meaning. It's written specifically for anyone ready to level up in their career and make a living doing something that brings them joy—blogging.

We're not just going to talk about how to blog (There's already enough out there about that!) but how to do it the *right way*. The way that will make you money without sucking all of your time, energy, and resources.

Yes, there is a wrong way to blog. At some point, even the most passionate blogger will get burned out when they realize they've turned their purpose-driven blog into another 9 to 5 job. The only way to avoid this is to learn *how to blog smarter, not harder*.

This book is not for hobby bloggers although there's nothing wrong with that. It also won't go in-depth about the basics of starting a blog although we do cover some basic terms, tips, and resources in Chapter 3. In fact, it's not even for people who want to start a blog as a side hustle.

This book is for the blogger who wants to turn their blog into a successful business.

This book is for the mother of two, who has journeyed through a rollercoaster in life and is ready to release her wisdom into the world, so she can contribute value to other people's lives. She wants to make enough money from her business to give her family an amazing life.

This book is also for the successful real estate professional, who's fed up with the system and tasted the joy of his own value reflecting itself back to him this year. He endeavored into a new venture on the side, and, naturally, it's blossoming as his career clarity is refined.

And, most importantly, this book is for you, whoever you are, reading this. You're here to learn, and that's exactly what will happen as you read this book.

What's the difference between a blogging business and a blog?

The difference is mostly the owner's *mindset*. It's a simple answer. But it makes all the difference in the world.

Believe it or not, becoming a blogger can suck your soul away, just like a job can. A blogging business is distinguished from a blog by its vision to scale as it grows, eventually removing its owner from the day-to-day work.

In Michael Gerber's book, *The E-Myth Revisited: Why Most Small Businesses Don't Work and What to Do About It*, the author explains three functional roles in a business owner's lifespan:

- Technician

- Manager

- Entrepreneur

The Technician *does all the work themselves.* The Manager *oversees the work* of subordinates. And the Entrepreneur *creates the vision for the business* and hires out the rest.

How does this look in the world of a blogger?

The Technician builds their own website, writes their own content, distributes their blog posts to available platforms (social media, search engines, etc.), outreaches to others to gain authority, gets backlinks, optimizes the design of their blog to maximize their monetization, and more.

The Manager researches and creates content calendars, hires writers, hires administrative help, and outsources all of the above work to a Technician to perform.

The Entrepreneur leads the operational team and collects the profits of the business.

Which one sounds the most like you? If you're anything like most people, you are probably a bit of all three. But you probably find yourself naturally drawn to one role more than the others.

What if I don't want to run a blogging business?

Great news! You don't have to run your blog as a business. We're not here to force you to become a business owner if that's not your goal.

But that is *the primary focus of this book*. Sure, you can be a Technician, still be happy, and even make a lot of money without taking the entrepreneurial approach.

But this book is for people who want to step out of the technician role and scale their blog into a successful business. If that sounds like you, keep reading.

Let's get started

Before we dive into all the tips and techniques to help you blog smarter, not harder, you need to make a few decisions.

Decision #1: Why are you blogging?

Sure, we can walk you through how to set up your website. We can talk about the best layout for your homepage or the best tools to do keyword research. But we'd be getting way ahead of ourselves if you haven't already answered decision #1: Why are you blogging in the first place?

There are a thousand things you can do with your life. Yet, you've decided to become a blogger. Why? What is it that entices you to choose this career path?

We're not asking for anything deep here—just that you're honest.

Do you want to make a lot of money? Do you want the freedom and autonomy that comes with entrepreneurship? Do you want to share an important message that helps other people?

There are likely multiple factors that have led you to a career in blogging. If you don't already know these reasons, spend some time ruminating on this question and write down your reasons.

Because at the end of the day, regardless of how successful you become, every single decision you make for yourself and your business will come back to your *why*.

Decision #2: What do you want to give?

Once you know why you want to be a blogger, you must make another big decision. What is it that you want to give to other people?

Blogging, at its core, is an exchange of value. The most successful bloggers know who they're talking to and how to communicate in ways that offer true value to their readers.

Content creation is the heart of blogging. You just have to decide what type of content you're going to share on your blog.

In general, there are three different types of bloggers: entertainers, educators, and influencers. Many blogs overlap in two or all of these categories, but most focus the majority of their content around one.

Simply put, *entertainers* give their readers entertainment. This form of media is especially common with video bloggers. Think of the husband and wife who post about the pranks they play on each other or a satire news blog.

Entertainment blogs often involve humor, but it's not essential. Blogs that recap popular television shows, sports blogs, and some book blogs would also be considered entertainment blogs.

Educators aim to teach their readers about a particular topic. This is a common blogging method in extremely niche blogs. If you've owned a lawn care company for several years and want to start writing about lawn care tips, then you're starting an education blog. You're educating your readers about a topic in which you have a lot of knowledge and/or experience.

Other examples of education blogs include food sites, tutorials, business, finance, and fitness blogs. Review blogs also fall into this category although they can overlap with influencer blogs as well.

Influencers aim to persuade their readers' perspectives, values, buying habits, or other decision-making factors.

When done right, these blogs also educate and inspire their readers to take positive action for themselves or others. When done wrong, they can have harmful influence on individuals and even societies.

Examples of influencer blogs include lifestyle, fashion, health and wellness, travel, and parenting. If your primary aim is to get readers to think or act differently, then you have an influencer blog.

Decision #3: What do you want to receive?

Relationships are reciprocal. Any union without reciprocity is not a relationship.

You're looking for a reciprocity with your blog, so you need to think not just about what it is that you want to give to your readers but what you want to get back.

- Do you want to feel a certain way? (Valuable, admired, important?)

- Are you hoping to make money?

- Is social impact your currency? (Do you want to influence and change the world?)

Let's say that what you want to give is education. You want to reach multitudes with the information they are looking for and supply it. You want to teach something you already know and help other people because of it.

But you also want to make money, and you've decided that dollars will be a quantitative metric for you to gauge your success.

The qualitative measure will be "How much I helped others." And you'll quantify it by seeing how much money you earn.

This is the water for your tree. It's the way you get fed. It's how you receive the energy and nourishment to keep offering value in the reciprocity of the relationship between you and your readers.

One important lesson

There are a dozen and one clichés about patience and time, but we're just going to say it simply. You will not become rich from blogging overnight.

It's extremely rare for bloggers, especially those who haven't yet built and grown a successful blog, to have immediate success. Many of us have had small and big wins, followed by small and big failures.

The key to success as a blogger (which you'll hear repeatedly in this book, it's that important!) is this: *Never give up.*

We interviewed successful bloggers for this book, all making more than six-figures a year, and every single one of them said *persistence* was the most important lesson they learned on their blogging journey.

Don't give up. Even if it takes a long time. Even if results don't come immediately. You're building an asset.

It's worth it because it will snowball. The beginning is the hardest part.

Our promise to you

In 2017, we dove headfirst into the world of online business. We had some major successes and some costly mistakes. Yet, over the course of three years, Wander Media grew into a six-figure blogging business.

With this book, our promise is that you will walk away feeling more confident than ever before about your blogging journey. We'll share the top tips and tricks we've used and what other successful bloggers have used to grow any blog into a successful business.

Here is what you can expect from this book:

- An overview, or refresher, of some of the blogging terms and tools that you *must know*

- Actionable tips that will help you grow your blog and make money

- An in-depth look at every blog monetization strategy and how to decide which ones are best for you

- Stories that will inspire you to achieve your goal of building a six-figure blogging business

- Common mistakes all bloggers make and how to avoid them

- Lessons on how to outsource (and why you shouldn't be afraid of it!)

- And much more!

Sound good to you? Awesome. Let's dive right in...

CHAPTER 2

The Past, the Present, and the Future of Blogging

Blogging is an integral part of internet culture. Even if someone doesn't know the term "blog," they've most definitely visited one if they've spent any time at all online.

In this chapter, we'll dive into what blogging is, how it came into being, what it looks like now, and how we believe it will evolve over time.

If you feel like you already know the basics, feel free to skip this chapter and head on to the next one. (However, personally we believe that there are nuggets of wisdom and knowledge here for those at any stage of their blogging journey. And it can never hurt to refresh your memory!)

What is blogging?

The site where you read "10 things Kylie Jenner does every morning"; the link you clicked to know the "Best smartphones under $500"; the website you visited to download your Thanksgiving meal grocery checklist.

All of it. All websites, excluding social media, from where you consume information and entertainment are considered blogs.

An even better definition, that is not exactly a definition, but gives an overview of blogging comes from George Siemens: "Where the Internet is about availability of information, blogging is about making information creation available to anyone."

Yes, that anyone can be *you*. In other words, you can be a blogger. And helping you become a successful one is our aim with this book.

History of blogging

The omnipresence of blogs—owned by individuals, small businesses, and corporations—is a truth of the modern age. However, blogging wasn't such a widely accepted concept in the early days. In the beginning, blogging was merely a way for people to share their daily life, thoughts, and perspectives.

So, how did blogging become the giant industry that it is today? That can be known by taking a look at its past. To understand its history, we have to go back to the mid-1990s, an era when many of the professional bloggers we know today were born (literally).

1994: More than two and a half decades ago, then 19-year-old Justin Hall created Links.net while he was an undergrad at Swarthmore College. It's recognized as the first blog, and Justin is considered the founding father of personal blogging.

Of course, it wasn't called blogging back then. As a matter of fact, there wasn't any particular term. People called it different things, including personal home page, online diary, and online journal.

1997: It wasn't until 1997 that a term for this online activity was coined. In December 1997, Jon Barger of *Robot Wisdom* termed it as 'weblog,' a made-up yet concise word to describe "logging the web/internet activity."

1998: *The Charlotte Observer* became a pioneer when Jonathan Dube blogged Hurricane Bonnie on the traditional news site.

Another pivotal point in the blogging space came in October of the same year when Open Diary was launched. Before Open Diary, blogging was a one-way street. Open Diary, with its community approach, allowed members to comment on others' work.

1999: The end of the millennium also marked another crucial year in the history of blogging. A programmer named Peter Merholz rebranded 'weblog' as 'blog', the term by which we know it today.

Many blogging platforms tried to push their products and services the same year. Among many, the Blogger platform (now owned by Google) and LiveJournal platform were the primary blogging platforms.

Blogger, in particular, has had a considerable influence in getting blogging in the mainstream. Another popular platform that has faded with time was Xanga.

2000s: The foundation was set in the '90s. The 2000s was the growth period. The number of people who started blogging grew exponentially. From mere tens of blogs in the '90s to almost 150 million blogs at the end of 2010, the growth was unreal.

2003: This year gave us the most successful and well-known blogging platform to date. Founder Matt Mullenweg launched Word-Press in 2003. Today, more than one-third of the internet is hosted by WordPress, and about two-thirds of the CMS market is acquired by it.

Another product that quite literally changed people's perception of blogging, Google's AdSense, launched in 2003. It was the first ad network that aimed to display relevant ads on blogs. As far as we're concerned, AdSense laid the foundation for what you're about to read in this book: making money online with blogging.

2004: By 2004, blogging was booming, thanks to new monetization methods surfacing on the market. Also, meta blogs—blogs about blogging—started popping up.

Another highlight of 2004—it was the year video blogs started. Sure, there were some video blogs before that, dating back to the year 2000. But 2004 was what we consider the establishment year of the "vlog."

Why do people blog?

Short answer: To make money—directly or indirectly, in the short term or long term.

Long answer: Though some people start a blog purely out of passion and discover monetization options later, many start out with a clear goal.

Individuals and professional bloggers do it to generate revenue via advertisements, affiliate marketing, sponsored posts, and more. (We will discuss all the monetization methods in a later chapter of this book.)

On the other hand, businesses consider blogging as part of their marketing strategy, specifically their content marketing strategy.

Overall, these are some of the primary reasons why people blog:

1. For self-expression and to share knowledge

Individuals blog to share their ideas and opinions on anything and everything. The motivations behind doing so can vary, such as:

- They want to voice their opinions and perhaps make a difference. You never know who could end up reading your blog post and how it could help them.

- They want to share their passion or knowledge.

- They want to connect with like-minded people.

- They want to hone their writing and communication skills.

Or, if it's none of these, blogging is a step with a clear business goal in mind.

2. Blogs act as ToFu content

In marketing terms, ToFu stands for Top-of-Funnel.

ToFu is about getting a potential customer in the sales cycle or buyer's journey. It's the awareness part or the entry point of a sales funnel. In other words, it's meant to bring as many new visitors as possible to the website and eventually turn them into leads and customers.

Blogging is a proven way to fulfill ToFu needs. It's a form of inbound marketing that attracts people. Again, the reason behind it can be anything. Often, blog posts answer people's questions or serve a specific need. Other times, they are purely entertainment or human interest.

All in all, one of the reasons why most businesses blog is because blogs get people into the buyer's journey.

3. To become an authority in the market

There are two people: Tom and Joe. Both sell pet supplies online.

Tom regularly posts articles related to his line of work. For example, articles on topics like, "Why X product will reduce your dog's hair loss" or "Top 5 toothbrushes for your cat." On the other hand, Joe just sits in his brick and mortar shop and expects someone to buy from his online store.

Who are you going to buy from if you come across both websites? Our guess is Tom. Why? Because you subconsciously look at Tom as the authority who knows what he is selling. Plus, he's already provided valuable information to you, so you trust him more.

This can be applied to any industry. The formula is simple: Showcase knowledge and expertise by posting relevant, timely, and high-quality content.

4. For writers, a blog is a portfolio

The writing industry is on the boom as more businesses get serious about the content on their sites.

For writers and authors, blogging on their blog or other authority blogs is a great way to showcase their writing style, expertise on the subject matter, and quality of their writing. It's among the best ways to find new clients and gain more exposure.

5. It gets businesses more sales

People who understand SEO and apply it better than competitors benefit a great deal from blogging. It's the primary source of organic traffic for most sites. By blogging, one can rank for relevant keywords and bring relevant traffic to their website.

Moreover, statistics show that SEO leads have a 14.6% close rate compared to 1.7% of outbound leads.

"SEO leads have a 14.6% close rate compared to 1.7% of outbound leads."

To explain it further, let's continue the previous Tom and Joe example.

If Tom's "Top 5 toothbrushes for your cat" article ranks for the key phrase "best toothbrushes for cats" and brings one thousand organic leads monthly, a 14.6% close rate means **146 people** will possibly buy a toothbrush from Tom's store.

Moreover, cross-sells and upsells will add more to that revenue. And if the customer likes the product, Tom gains a lifelong customer!

In a nutshell, it goes to show the effect of blogging on the bottom line.

6. It's a way to connect on a personal level

People love stories. And many businesses use blogging as a tool to amplify the stories that connect with customers and other people on an emotional level.

Let us share an example. Say you run a web agency that builds websites and apps for your clients. Sophia is the UX designer responsible for the fantastic experience of sites your clients as well as their customers love. Interviewing her or highlighting her contributions via the company blog will connect with everyone on a personal level.

1. Sophia feels appreciated. **Benefit**: She is more likely to want to stay with the company long-term.

2. Such blogs encourage potential employees to apply if the company is recruiting. **Benefit**: It improves the employer's brand.

3. Clients and potential clients see the company as more than something that sends the invoice once the job is done. **Benefit**: Long-lasting business relations.

It's just one example. A blog can highlight anyone from a janitor or a supplier to the CEO and build the same connection.

7. It helps in keeping other online channels active

Blog content can be repurposed for other online channels. This way, one can stay relevant and consistent throughout the internet.

- A quote from the blog post can be shared in image form on Instagram and Pinterest. The same quote can be tweeted as well.

- A summary of the article can be published on a Facebook page or LinkedIn.

- It can be used as a base of the script for a YouTube video.

- Multiple blog posts can be combined to create an e-book or other type of lead generation offer.

- The whole article can be republished on third-party platforms, like Quora, Medium, and LinkedIn Pulse.

- It can help you keep in touch with your email subscribers.

Overall, consistent blogging fuels your entire content strategy.

8. To make money online

Most of the mentioned points are indirectly related to making money. Those are relevant to businesses that have products or services to sell. This point considers the blog as the product.

Most professional bloggers create niche blogs and make money by selling advertising space on the blog, accepting sponsored posts, or placing affiliate links wherever relevant.

For them, at the most basic level, it's a four-step process:

- Create content people will want to read.

- Optimize the content for search engines.

- Get as much traffic as possible.

- Make money by displaying others' messages/products/services on the blog.

The points above encapsulate almost all reasons why people blog. We feel these will remain the primary objectives of blogging in the future.

However, blogging in itself won't always stay the same.

The future of blogging

Let's address the elephant in the room first. Is blogging dead or going to die?

Judging by the ever-increasing number of blogs and blog readers, blogging is perfectly safe. Yes, people skim through blog posts, but does that mean they do not read blogs? Absolutely not!

The better question to ask is, "How will blogging evolve in the future? And what should I do to stay ahead?"

Here are our predictions:

1. The future is creative

A recent headline on The Verge read: "A college student used GPT-3 to write fake blog posts and ended up at the top of Hacker News."

The subheading was, "He says he wanted to prove the AI could pass as a human writer."

As it appears, it did. And with development in AI, ML, and Big Data, it'll get better and better. So, the unoriginal and rephrased writing that works today for some bloggers won't in the future.

However, if you have new ideas, new perspectives, a different approach that touches the human mind and heart, or anything that feeds your creative brain, you are future-proof as a blogger.

In short, the best blogging is all about being human. Machines won't ever replicate that.

2. The future is in authority blogging

Google allegedly manipulates search results and favors big brands over small brands—in blogging terms, a big website over a small site. You may have noticed that sites like Quora, Medium, and Linke-dIn dominate SERPs.

So, how do you convince the algorithm to put your blog at the top of search results? Authority blogging. Google prefers authority sites. So be one.

Google's mantra is to provide the best answer on the internet. And if you provide it, sooner or later, you will succeed.

Our advice? Focus on one niche and become the authority. How? Focus on quality content.

3.   *The future is in content marketing*

Most traditional bloggers blog with a single purpose—to make money. The goal with this mentality is simple: Get traffic to your blog and convert that traffic via sales, affiliate marketing, or other monetization methods.

However, if you're serious about making a full-time income from blogging and living the digital nomad lifestyle, you need to think like a content marketer.

If you don't know what content marketing is, this definition from CMI is perfect: "Content marketing is a strategic marketing approach focused on creating and distributing valuable, relevant, and consistent content to attract and retain a clearly defined audience and, ultimately, to drive profitable customer action."

As a content marketer, you look at blog posts mostly as a top of the funnel content. You use it to drive traffic, collect leads, and then sell via email, retargeting, and so on. Indeed, you can keep earning from the traditional method, but this makes your income source future-proof.

4. *The future is in advertising*

Even with roughly one million monthly page sessions, there are some affiliate blogs earning over $100,000 per month. In blog-o-speak, that's an RPM of $100.

That's important because at a per-site-visitor ratio, advertising doesn't make nearly that much money. It's certainly possible with e-commerce websites to make this much.

But in the future, it's likely that algorithms and big data will reverse this. Why?

The selective choices that blog owners are making are rational, calculated choices.

- Which products to create

- Which affiliate partnerships to promote to their audience

In a future where algorithms know us better than we know ourselves—and certainly better than bloggers know their audience—these choices will be handed over to artificial intelligence.

In short, AI will be able to link to a product or service that is of greater value to the individual reader than the product the blogger will choose.

Rather than products, services, and offerings being selected by humans for their audience (aggregate data, generalized experience), in the future, the RPMs for blogging will be highest for pure advertising sites.

How do you future-proof your blog?

Again, it all comes back to content. Algorithms and best practices for monetization will change many times over the years.

The best way to future-proof your blog is to focus on quality content. Content is the foundation of the blogging world.

Here are a few things you can do:

- Keep creating the best content you can

- Write authentically

- Become an expert in your niche

- Stay up-to-date with blogging and SEO trends and changes

- Don't focus on topics that don't matter to you

Remember that when we look to the future, we don't know. We must admit our own frailty to imagine all the possibilities.

CHAPTER 3

Blogging 101: What Every Blogger Needs to Know

Now that you know the evolution of blogging and what lies ahead in the industry, it's time to get your hands dirty.

By "hands dirty," we do not intend to ask you to do the menial work. Remember, this book is all about how to blog smarter, not harder. We merely mean understanding some of the common terms and concepts before getting started. Blogging 101, to be precise.

Common lingo

You're about to enter the blogosphere. It's a sphere or a planet of sorts. And the lingo—words, phrases, etc.—used by the people who reside here is unique.

Just kidding (kind of). Learn the following commonly used blogging terms, and you're good to go.

- **AdSense:** AdSense is Google's ad network. Bloggers can sign up with AdSense to display advertisements on their site.

- **Alt tag:** Alt tag, short for alternative tag, is an HTML tag applied to images added on a blog. Two major reasons to use alt tags include 1.) the SEO benefit and 2.) If the image is broken, the text will take the place of the image to set some context for the visitor.

- **Affiliate:** A blogger who monetizes their blog by promoting another brand's products or services in exchange for a commission is called an affiliate marketer.

- **Avatar:** An avatar simply means the profile picture the blogger uses to represent himself or herself online. It's typically found beside the author's name in the blog's bio section.

- **Analytics:** Any data gathered about a blog (mostly represented in a graphical manner) is considered analytics. Depending on the context, by "analytics," a blogger can also mean Google Analytics, the leading website analytics tool.

- **Anchor text:** The anchor text is the visible text on which a hyperlink to another and mostly relevant web page is placed.

- **Blogosphere:** The collective of all the blogs on the internet is the blogosphere.

- **Bots:** Bots are automated entities often used to spam comments on blogs or social media.

- **Bounce rate:** The bounce rate is the ratio of the number of people who visited your website to the total number of pages the visitor viewed. E.g., if 100 people visited 200 web pages on your site, the bounce rate is 50%. In general, the lower the bounce rate, the better.

- **Backlink:** A backlink is gained when an external website hyperlinks back to your site.

- **Category:** If there are multiple topics of discussion on the blog, they are categorized for user experience and SEO. E.g., if you run a tech products-related blog, two of the categories can be "Android" and "iOS."

- **Canonical link:** A canonical link or "rel=canonical" is a way to show search engines that the content on that particular page is duplicate content. This prevents SEO problems.

- **Clickbait:** If we go by the literal meaning, clickbait is a form of false advertisement. It's a way to get people to open or click on a link by means of misleading text, title, or graphic.

- **CMS:** A content management system (CMS) is software used for creation, modification, and management of digital content. The most popular CMS is WordPress.

- **Content marketing:** Content marketing is a form of marketing that involves all the aspects of the content, from creation to distribution.

- **Conversion rate:** The conversion rate is the ratio of the number of people who performed the desired task to the total number of people who visited the blog. E.g., if 10 out of 100 people who visited a landing page subscribed to the newsletter, the conversion rate is 10%.

- **CPC:** The cost per click (CPC) is the price advertisers are willing to pay for every click they receive on their ad on your blog.

- **CTA:** The CTA, or call-to-action, is anything a blogger adds to compel visitors to take a specific action. For example, a "Download Now" button you click on to download an e-book is considered a CTA.

- **CTR:** Also known as click through rate, the CTR is the percentage of people who clicked on the CTA after visiting the page.

- **DA/DR:** The Domain Authority (DA) and Domain Rating (DR) are metrics created by Moz's and Ahrefs's SEO tools, respectively. Basically, both quantify the authority and quality of a blog by rating it on a numerical score between one and 100. The higher the score, the better the rating.

- **Event blogging:** A type of blogging done to attract visitors during a specific event and hopefully make a profit out of it.

- **Evergreen content:** Unlike the content of event blogging, evergreen content is in-depth content that stays relevant over time.

- **Favicon:** It's the image, typically a variation of the blog's logo, that's seen by the readers in the address or title bar beside the blog's title.

- **Guest blogging:** Guest blogging is when you publish your content on someone else's blog in order to spread awareness, get traffic, and/or get backlinks.

- **Influencer:** Any blogger who has a large audience and any sort of influence over them is considered an influencer. Brands want to collaborate with those bloggers to promote their offerings.

- **Internal link:** A link from one page of the blog to another page of the same blog is an internal link.

- **Keyword:** A word or a phrase that best describes the content of the blog and that readers typically search for is a keyword.

- **Listicle:** A listicle is the term used to describe a list-based blog post style. E.g., if this section were a blog post, we'd title it "45+ common words/phrases used by bloggers," and it would be a listicle.

- **Lead magnet:** A lead magnet, also called a lead generation offer, is something exclusive offered by a blogger to get visitors to join their email list. Lead magnets usually offer value to the subscriber and can be e-books, infographics, case studies, and more.

- **Media kit:** A media kit is a collection of all the relevant statistics about the blog and its audience. It's developed for potential sponsors of the blog so they can see what they're investing in.

- **Meta description:** The meta description tag in HTML includes a snippet summarizing the content of a web page. Search engines display it to the visitors to give an overview of what they'll read inside the post.

- **Nofollow:** A link with "rel=nofollow" is used to tell search engines to ignore that link.

- **Niche:** A blog niche is a topic you will be focusing on and creating content around. E.g., one of our blogs is about books, so we publish book reviews and listicles about books in different categories.

- **Newsletter:** A newsletter is the content sent out via email to the people who subscribed to your email list.

- **Organic:** Organic is a word used in place of non-paid. E.g., if the blog's traffic comes through search engine results, you didn't pay for that traffic. Hence, it's organic traffic.

- **Page views:** Page views equal the number of visitors on a particular page in a specific period of time.

- **PPC:** PPC is more of an advertising term than a blogging term, but sometimes bloggers also need to advertise. PPC, or pay per click, is the amount you pay for each click on an ad.

- **Permalink:** The URL you see in the address bar when you visit a web page is the permalink.

- **Pillar content:** Pillar content is an in-depth piece on a topic that can be divided into subtopics and many blog posts. E.g., if this book were a blog post, it would be pillar content because every chapter and every sub-topic can be a different blog post.

- **ROI:** ROI, or return on investment, is the ratio of net profit to the total investment.

- **RSS feed:** RSS is a web feed that allows users and applications to access updates to websites in a standardized, computer-readable format.

- **SERP:** It's short for search engine results page, which defines itself.

- **SEO:** It's short for search engine optimization, which also defines itself. SEO is a collection of methods used by bloggers to rank their posts higher on SERPs.

- **Slug:** The slug is the part of the URL that you typically see after the website's domain which identifies the exact page.

- **Syndication:** Syndication is a method of republishing blog content on other websites with the goal of reaching more people.

- **WYSIWYG:** It's the abbreviation for "what you see is what you get." Typically, it is used when designing your website using a visual builder. In that context, it means the way your site looks while you build is the way it will look once built.

- **Yoast:** Yoast SEO is a popular WordPress plugin used for search engine optimization.

These are the terms that will be thrown around in the blogging communities if you wish to join one. So, you better know it beforehand rather than go searching for the meaning every time you don't understand something.

Research: Know your audience, niche, and competitors

Up until now, you've read about the industry we all know as blogging. Now it's time to take a deep breath and think—think about whether you want to enter this oversaturated, yet full of opportunities, industry. Calm down. Think!

Do you have a clear answer? Is that answer 'yes'? Well, then, it's time to dive even deeper. Reading up until now was just an introduction to the blogosphere. Next up, we'll talk about what topic, or niche, you want to serve.

And to help you understand the importance of research and inspire you a bit, here's an anonymous, but accurate, quote: "In today's complex and fast-moving world, what we need even more than foresight or hindsight is insight."

1. Find your niche and understand it inside out

As mentioned earlier, *a blog niche is a topic you will be focusing on and creating content around.* It's something you must—and we mean MUST—be serious about. It's so crucial.

You might have read this quote somewhere on Instagram: "Direction is so much more important than speed. Many are going nowhere fast." As cliché as it may sound, it applies to blogging. Your niche is your direction. And you should choose it wisely. If you don't, you may run out of fuel early and/or make no money/make a financial/ time loss.

2. Choosing a niche

If we remove all the fluff around this topic, choosing the niche boils down to four key things—an ikigai of sorts, if you may:

- Areas you love

- Topics you are good at

- An audience for the subject at present and in the future

- A niche that pays well

3. Filtering the topics

To find the ideal niche, you need to filter out the topics you aren't interested in. This will leave you with ones you are either passionate about or know about—if both, even better! Brainstorm and list all of them in a Word document.

To help you even further, here are some great niches we have found while researching for our blogs:

- Health
- Fitness
- Dating
- Skincare
- Haircare
- Cars
- Motorcycles
- Cooking and recipes
- Crafts/DIY
- Home improvement
- Personal finance
- Investing
- Make money online (or MMO)
- Marketing
- Business
- eCommerce
- Crypto
- Education
- Language
- Fashion
- Exercise
- Yoga
- Gardening

- Personal development
- Pets and animal care
- Books
- Gadgets
- Technology
- IT
- Web development and design
- Graphic design
- Travel
- Sports
- eSports
- Wedding
- Music
- Musical instruments
- Movies
- Parenting
- Career advice
- Farming

These are some of the niches of blogs we come across day in and day out. Moreover, all the mentioned topics are too broad. Literally, thousands of microniches or sub-niches can be created from this list alone.

E.g., a blog specific to pianos, guitars, or violins can be created rather than one on all musical instruments. Similarly, a blog focusing on SEO, PPC, or Facebook makes more sense than a blog on marketing.

All in all, list all the niches and microniches of your interest in a document.

4. Right next to that, make a column "Audience"

In this column, describe your core audience as per the niche. This may include audience:

- Size
- Demographic
- Gender
- Location
- Spending
- Interests

The main factor you need to look at here is the size of the audience. Is it substantial enough? Because if you are going to write reviews of expensive cellos only, the audience might be pretty tiny.

The best way to find the audience size is by looking at the number of searchers for the top keywords in the niche. You can use tools, like Google Keyword Planner, Ahrefs, or KWFinder, for it.

5. Another column to add is "Competition"

Right at the beginning, we mentioned blogging is an oversaturated industry. This doesn't mean that you can't be found at the top, though. There are opportunities for everyone.

In the "Competition" column, mark each niche with the level of competition—very low, low, medium, high, very high.

To determine which niche belongs to which category, there are a couple of methods.

1. Search for the keywords that pop in your mind when you think about the niche. Look at the top-ranking sites. This will give you a general idea about the kind of competition you will be up against. For instance, if the top articles are from the likes of Forbes, Entrepreneur, Techcrunch, or WebMD, the competition is very high.

2. Look at the average DA or DR of the sites that frequently come up on top SERPs. If it's 80+, it's very high competition; 60+ is high; 40+ is medium; and below 30 is low.

Now that you have categorized the competition level, we'd suggest eliminating the 'high' and 'very high' at the initial level. Also, 'very low' competition means there's not much to gain there. This leaves you with low to medium-level competitors.

6. Finally, look at the business value of the niches

Let's not kid ourselves here. Most of us are in it to make money. So, it's vital to know the business value—the kind of money you will make if you succeed. The most quantifiable way to recognize the importance of any niche is by the CPC.

The last column to add on that sheet is "CPC". It's the price advertisers are willing to pay for every click on their ad they get from your blog. E.g., If you run a blog around, say, insurance, or legal services, the CPC will be in the tens of dollars. On the other hand, if you blog about electronics, the CPC will be under a dollar.

Another factor that determines the business value of your niche is the geographic location of your target audience. For example, the average CPC in India is 77% less than the US average. So, yes, you must choose your target audience wisely. We know we are repeating ourselves here, but it's just that crucial!

This is the most common way of quantifying the possible value of a niche. If you're going to build an audience and sell a product/service or run your blog on a subscription model, then the earning potential will be in that context obviously.

To wrap it up, let's summarize it all in a word. RESEARCH!

Understanding SEO

Organic search has been, is, and will be a vital source of traffic for blogs. That's a fact. Another fact—a statistic from an Ahrefs's study, actually—is that 91% of web pages never get any traffic from Google.

This means if you want to get organic traffic, your web page (where you'd like organic traffic to go) needs to be among the top 9% mathematically. Ideally, for substantial traffic, you need to be in the top 1%. And before you start questioning yourself, let us tell you it's plausible. How? One term: SEO.

To define SEO, we'd like to quote a very accurate definition by Moz. "SEO stands for 'search engine optimization'. It's the practice of increasing both the quality and quantity of website traffic, as well as exposure to your brand, through non-paid, also known as 'organic', search engine results."

To understand SEO a bit clearer, let's divide it into three primary parts:

- On-page SEO
- Off-page SEO
- Technical SEO

We can categorize it even further, like White Hat SEO or Black Hat SEO. However, these three will cover most things.

On-page SEO

On-page SEO (or on-site SEO) refers to the techniques/changes one implements on their web pages and site to rank it better.

It's essentially a significant part of telling, "Hey, Google Algorithm, come look at me. I am relevant and high-quality. I am the best answer to the searcher's query."

On-page optimization is a mix of techniques you can control, such as:

- *URL Structure*

A well-crafted URL shows search engines and humans what the page is about. For example, instead of *example.com/page/1234*, if the web address is *example.com/what-is-url-structure*, the probability of the latter one ranking over the first one is higher.

- *Content Structure*

Not only is a well-formatted blog post easy on the eye, but it also helps search engine crawlers understand the content. Therefore, use headings and sub-headings wherever usable. A properly structured article will also decrease the bounce rate and increase average session time, i.e., it will indirectly affect SEO.

- *Keywords*

Keywords are the words or phrases you want to rank your web page for. And everything in regards to it is in your control, right from finding relevant keywords using keyword research tools to sprinkling those keyword(s) appropriately in your content, meta description, and meta tags.

- *Title tags*

The title tag is an HTML element that's used to tell the search engine what title to display. If used well—with primary keyword(s) in it—it can be extremely beneficial in rankings.

- *Website speed*

Another factor that widely affects your search engine position and is in your control is website speed. You can optimize your website speed by choosing a high-performing web host, optimization plugins, CDN, a better CMS, and so on.

- *Inter-linking*

Relevantly linking one page of your blog to another page can also affect search engine ranking in a teeny-tiny manner. Besides, it will also decrease the bounce percentage and increase the overall time spent by the reader on the site. This means it will positively affect ranking indirectly, too.

These are some of the facets of on-page SEO you need to know. There's much more to it, and we will discuss it in our SEO book if we decide to publish one. Until then, let's move on to the next category.

Off-page SEO

Off-page SEO deals with the external factors that influence your search engine rankings. It's perhaps the largest contributor to a site's E-A-T factor. *E-A-T stands for expertise, authoritativeness, and trustworthiness. It's Google's way of measuring the quality of a web page.*

At the heart of off-page SEO are backlinks, brand mentions, and social signals.

-   *Backlinks*

As we already mentioned in our glossary, *a backlink is a hyperlink from another site to your site.*

When another site links to your blog post, it tells Google that your post is relevant to the topic/heading/sub-heading/anchor text of that web page, and it is worthy enough to be linked/referred to.

The impact on a backlink on your site ranking for your keyword depends on numerous factors:

-   The anchor text.
-   Relevancy of your page in relation to the linking page.

- The authority of the site linking to your blog. E.g., If the DR of that site is 80+, its impact on the ranking is much higher than many links from websites with DR 20-30s combined.

- The authority of that particular page of the site.

- Is it "dofollow" or "nofollow"?

- *Brand mentions*

When another site mentions your brand, it also has a slight impression on your rankings.

For example, In an article about blogging, if someone mentions "Wander Media," Google adds it to its knowledge graph. For Google's algorithm, it means Wander Media is related to blogging in some form. And if someone adds a link to our site on that anchor, a brand mention and backlink is even better.

- *Social signals*

Search engine crawlers also collect the data from social media sites—the number of times the article was shared on Twitter, Facebook, Pinterest, and so forth.

So, yes, adding a CTA that encourages the readers to share it on social media can increase your chances of getting to top SERPs.

Technical SEO

Technical SEO ensures that your site and its pages/posts/categories are indexable and crawlable by the search engine crawlers.

On top of that, managing elements, such as mobile-friendliness, site architecture, site navigation, rendering, breadcrumbs, loading speed, duplicate content (add "noindex" tag), robot.txt file, and XML sitemaps is a part of technical SEO.

In most cases, you won't need to dive into technical SEO. Still, having an understanding of the technical SEO factors can be beneficial.

Long story short, if you create quality content and apply your on-page, off-page, and technical SEO understanding to it, you will rank on top SERPs unless your competitors are doing it better.

Building a content calendar

At the heart of blogging, SEO, marketing, or any search engine algorithm is content. Therefore, it must be your priority.

If you want to turn your blog(s) into a high-income source, adding content when you feel like it won't work. You have to look at it as a business. And no business succeeds without a proper strategy.

Our advice: Make a content schedule and stick to it!

What is a content calendar?

A content calendar is a visual workflow that helps your team of virtual assistants, writers, editors, and other contractors schedule, plan, or organize their work on a daily, weekly, monthly, or quarterly basis. (*We didn't mention a team earlier, did we? Well, don't worry. There's a whole chapter on it—why you need one and how to hire.*)

As for an ideal content calendar, there's no one-size-fits-all. It depends on a number of things, including the frequency of posting, the filtering it goes through, the type of content (for the blog, social media, newsletter, etc.), the time the graphic designer needs to create the cover image, and much more.

Anyway, one thing can be common in any content/editorial schedule. The tool(s) used.

Tools to build a content calendar

There are many premium and free content calendar tools in the market, including KanbanFlow, StoryChief, Flow-e, GatherContent, Asana, and Monday. You might have heard some names if you have ever looked for project management tools.

Our favorite and the ones we recommend are basic and free ones: Google Sheets or a project management tool, like Trello.

- *Google Sheets*

Google Sheets is a web-based spreadsheet program, just like Microsoft's Excel. We have used it on multiple occasions to smoothen our editorial and scheduling process.

Let us share the most basic way we've used it as a content calendar. We created a sheet and shared it with all of our writers, editors, and VAs working on the blog. These were the columns we added:

- Month
- Post Title

- Writer
- Status (Assigned, Editing, Draft, Scheduled, Published)
- Writer Deadline
- Target Publish Date
- Primary Keyword
- Additional Keywords
- Average Monthly Search Volume
- Keyword Difficulty
- Notes/Description
- Number of Words
- Payment status

It's a simple spreadsheet that works very well as a content calendar. You can also connect the Google Sheet with Google Calendar and invite your freelancers/employees there. That's a non-mandatory extra step, though.

Bonus: We created a FREE Content Calendar Template just for you. You can find the template on EinsteinBlogging.com.

- *A project management tool*

Any quality project management tool can work seamlessly to create a content calendar and collaborate with people related to the project. Some of the fantastic tools for the job are Asana, JIRA, Airtable, ClickUp, Basecamp, and Trello.

We personally use Trello, so we'll continue with our example.

Trello is a widely popular project management tool that we use to maintain a content calendar. You can add up to 10 members on the free version. For more members and extra features & functionalities, you can upgrade to either the Business Class or Enterprise plan.

We use the free version, which works perfectly fine. Here's the step-by-step way to create a content calendar on Trello:

1. Create a board. Title it *Content Calendar* or whatever you want.

2. In it, you'll have the option to "Add a list". Create as many as you need to—we have lists for content ideas, content titles, pipeline, drafts, editing, ready to publish, and published ones.

3. In each list, create cards. A "card" can contain an outline/description, a due date, checklist, attachments, and so on. Once ready, tag the writers associated with the card in its description. This way, the writer will get a notification about the assigned project and due date.

   Apart from it, you can drag and drop the cards across the lists. For instance, if an article is edited, it can be pulled from the "Editing" list and placed in the "Ready to publish" one.

That's all about Trello, creating a content calendar, and this fundamentals chapter.

Now, it's time to get to the meat of what the book title promises: the smart way of blogging and making money. We'll be sharing some re-al-life examples and tips and techniques to scale your blog and how to make money with blogs in general.

But first, a disclaimer

You're about to consume a lot of foundational blogging knowledge that if grasped and applied should guarantee HUGE success for your blogging business.

It will take focus. But don't worry if you forget things. You can al-ways refer to this book as a helpful resource when the time comes.

You may feel like some of the topics are too high-level for where you are currently at on your blogging journey. Don't let this overwhelm you. Even if you don't fully grasp all of the concepts initially, our goal is that this information gives you a solid foundation so when you get to the point where you're ready to apply these tactics in the real world, you can circle back to these chapters for insight and per-spective.

Keep this book on your desk, or on your desktop if you have the dig-ital version, so you can easily reference it as you work on growing your blog.

Ready to feed your mind with some high-value blogging informa-tion? Take a short break if you need to, get a glass of water, and let's go...

CHAPTER 4

How to Make Money from Blogging

For this chapter, keep this fundamental premise at the fore-front of your mind:

> *Every business in existence requires **the sale of a product or service** (We'll just call these "goods" for the remainder of this chapter.).*

In the business of blogging, it's easy to lose sight of this reality. But losing sight of what you're selling will effectively cripple your strategy.

You might, unknowingly, leave a lot of money on the table.

How much money can you make from blogging?

The big question people want to know is, How much money can I actually make from my blog?

The answer to this questions depends on several factors:

- What is the purpose of your blog?

- How do you plan to monetize your blog?

- How much time and money can you invest in your blog?

The more you treat your blog like a business rather than a hobby, the higher your earning potential becomes.

Hobby bloggers are those who typically blog on the side while maintaining a full-time job or are not particularly interested in making a lot of money from blogging. Hobby bloggers tend to make anywhere from $0 to $2,000 per month from their blog.

However, if you want your blog to become a full-time business, there is potential for you to earn more than $25,000 per month from your blog. Not only can your blog replace your full-time job, if that is the goal, but blogging can make you *very rich*.

But to become a successful blogger, you first need to determine your business model.

Your blogging business model

Determining your business model boils down to asking yourself if you want to be marketing other people's goods, your own goods, or both. There are three common business models in blogging:

- Blogging Business Model #1: The Marketer *(Marketing others' goods)*

- Blogging Business Model #2: The Creator of Goods *(Marketing your own goods)*

- Blogging Business Model #3: The Dual Role *(Marketing both)*

Producing and marketing your own goods provides the highest potential for revenue *per website visitor.* This is because you are entirely vertically integrated. And you control pricing and don't have to rely on anyone else to market your goods.

The linchpin is this: Because profit equals long-term sustainability (and profits demand that expenses be *less than* revenue), marketing expenses are *always* less than gross sales revenue.

If you're exclusively a Marketer, then you always must be paid less (per website visitor) than the Creator of Goods because you're in their expense line item.

Does this make sense? Here's an illustration.

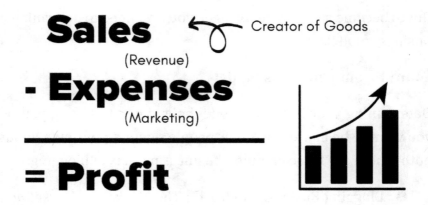

This doesn't mean that if you create goods, you automatically have a higher profit than someone who markets.

The Marketer can generate revenue from thousands of products, and even if they only earn a slice of the pizza pie (affiliate commissions, for example), they may earn 10,000 slices of pizza whereas the Creator of Goods may only sell five pizzas.

This is why some of the most successful bloggers don't produce goods, like our friends Ben and Jeff at DollarSprout (You'll read their story in Chapter 10.). They focus exclusively on marketing others' products.

At the end of the day, there is not one model that is inherently better than the others. What is more important than the model you choose is how you implement it. But before we get into that, let's dive into the key elements you need to understand when it comes to making money from blogging.

The big picture

Remember, blogs are marketing *assets* that drive traffic *towards a good.*

→ If the blog reader converts and purchases a good, then the Creator of Goods generates revenue.

→ If a reader *doesn't* convert to a purchaser, then the Creator of the goods does not generate revenue.

And like we've discussed, the blogger can still generate revenue from readers who don't convert to purchasers through marketing other people's goods.

So, ultimately as a blogger, and owner of a blogging business, you have to decide if you want to be the Creator of Goods, Marketer of Goods, or the Dual Role.

One piece of good news is this: You can always start with as a Marketer or Creator of Goods and move into the Dual Role down the road. You are not trapped to the role you decide on when you first start blogging, but you should always consider how your decisions as a blog owner fit into your long-term monetization strategy.

The big variable in this equation (conversion rate)

The seesaw between website traffic and revenue is called the conversion rate.

The conversion rate answers the question: What percentage of website visitors, when given the opportunity, will actually purchase a good?

Out of 1,000 website visitors, if 10 of them convert to customers, then the conversion rate is 1% (10 divided by 1,000).

Bloggers can increase their conversion rates by implementing an effective marketing strategy and creating the perception of a high value good. (Of course, if your good is actually of high value, it will be easier to sell. Never underestimate the strength of word-of-mouth marketing!)

Effective marketing tactics include:

- Directing the attention of website visitors to your goods

- Increasing visibility of your goods by way of promotion through email, social media, etc.

- Creating compelling copy and design that increases the value perception of your goods

Ultimately, there are many more components of an effective marketing strategy. For example, you'll want to make sure that you're targeting the right audience (the alignment of the good with the proper audience).

Marketing is, to an extent, manipulation. By manipulating, we don't mean lying to your potential customers. We mean controlling the narrative and enhancing the value perception of your goods through tactics like testimonials and positive reviews.

Revenue: The lifeblood of your blogging business

You already know that it's possible to make a lot of money from blogging. So, now we'll break down the specific ways you can generate revenue as a Marketer, Creator of Goods, or both.

In the blogging world, revenue is produced in multiple ways:

- Affiliate marketing

- E-commerce

- Display ads

- Sponsorships

- Paid membership

While some bloggers focus on just one method, like affiliate marketing, and still make a lot of money, many bloggers choose to use a hybrid model of monetization.

How do you determine what method is most profitable? The most common way to determine the value of your strategy is to look at *how much revenue is created per 1,000 page sessions of web traffic.*

This is called revenue per mille (RPM), and it's how bloggers determine the efficiency of each revenue stream.

Resources (money and time) should be invested into content that generates the highest RPMs.

For example, If your blog gets 10,000 sessions per month and generates $750 in revenue each month, your RPM is $75, which is *exceptionally* above average, by the way.

The equation looks like this:

(total revenue/total website sessions) x 1,000 = RPM

Some monetization methods tend to have higher earning potential than others. However, the higher the RPM, the more resources are typically required from the blogger.

Affiliate marketing

Through affiliate marketing, you promote another person's goods for a percentage of profit.

For example, if you add an affiliate link to another blogger's course in your blog post, and someone clicks that link and purchases the course, you get a small commission for influencing the sale.

Affiliate marketing is a popular method for beginner bloggers because it's relatively easy to set up and maintain, especially when compared to creating your own goods. However, while it's easy to get started with affiliate marketing, to get the most value from this model, you have to invest time in an effective affiliate marketing strategy and develop content focused on your readers' needs.

Without an effective affiliate marketing strategy, the earning potential is relatively low. However, with an effective strategy in place, the potential to make money from affiliate marketing can be extremely high. It's not unheard of for bloggers to make six-figures per month almost exclusively from affiliate commissions.

With affiliate marketing, there are no limits to what you can earn, and payouts for some goods can be extremely high. However, there are still risks involved.

The biggest risk of overreliance on this strategy comes from the lack of control you have over the commission structure. For example, in April of 2020, Amazon changed their commission structure for pet products from 8% per sale to 3%. This change had a huge impact on pet bloggers who relied on Amazon affiliate revenue as their primary source of income.

It should also be noted that because it's so easy to get started with affiliate marketing, you are competing with several other affiliate marketers, and typically you only get paid if someone actually makes a purchase.

Affiliate marketing is a fantastic way to earn money from blogging, and it's one that nearly all successful bloggers recommend. But it's vital to understand the risks of relying too heavily on a single affiliate program, like Amazon, as well as the importance of investing time in a solid affiliate marketing strategy.

E-commerce

This is where you sell products via an online storefront. You can create and sell your own products, or you can resell existing products at a high profit margin.

Compared to other monetization methods, e-commerce is more difficult to start and can potentially take up much more of your time. But when done right, the earning potential with e-commerce is extremely high.

When it comes to e-commerce, there are varying levels of difficulty. If you are creating your own products, physical products will typically be more expensive and time-consuming to create and manage than digital products. For example, creating a 300-page physical book is more difficult than creating a 10-page e-book.

While creating your own products requires a large upfront investment of resources, they do not require much time or money to maintain once the product is created. The exception in this case is if your good is a service, such as coaching or copywriting.

The largest benefits of having an e-commerce business are that you have full control over what you sell, and of course, you can *make a lot of money*. Many e-commerce business owners set up their own affiliate programs to encourage other bloggers to market their goods.

While successful goods can bring in a great deal of revenue, the e-commerce method isn't for everyone. Maintaining an e-commerce store can take a lot of time. You will likely have to deal with customer service issues. And if you don't have a solid marketing plan in place, there is no guarantee that your goods will be successful.

Display advertising

You know those ad boxes that you see on so many websites? Those are called display ads.

As a blogger, you can earn money when your website visitors view and click on those ads from your website. Like affiliate marketing, display advertising is one of the easiest ways to monetize your website.

Another perk of display advertising is that it requires a relatively low time commitment. Once you set up the ads on your site, you can start earning with fairly little maintenance required.

Many bloggers choose to work with ad networks. Ad networks help bloggers make more money from display advertising. Most networks require the blogger to apply and meet a set of criteria before they can join, such as having a certain amount of monthly visitors.

The benefits of joining an ad network are huge. Ad networks help pair bloggers with advertisers who pay good money to be featured on relevant websites. Working with an ad network will generally result in higher RPMs for the blogger than trying to set up display ads on your own.

Ad networks will often provide resources and support to help bloggers set up their pages for maximum RPM. Once you've optimized your pages, little maintenance is required on your part as the blogger. You get to continue to create content while enjoying a steady stream of income from advertising.

This makes display advertising one of the most passive ways to earn money from blogging. However, bloggers should be aware of several risks.

For one, the revenue you make from advertising correlates with the amount of traffic that comes to your blog. For example, you can't decide to stop blogging and continue to make the same amount of money from display advertising. You're also relying on what rates advertisers decide to pay for placing ads on your site.

For example, when the coronavirus pandemic resulted in the reduction of air travel, many travel bloggers suffered. Not only were fewer people visiting their blogs, but travel companies cut their advertising budgets. These factors resulted in travel bloggers earning much less from display ads than they were prior to the pandemic.

Another con of display advertising is that it can disrupt the user experience. According to a 2018 survey by Janrain, 41.7% of U.S. adults said display ads are "too aggressive" while another 18.6% acknowledge that display ads seem to understand their interests and needs but are creepy.

Display advertising can be an easy and effective way to make money from blogging, but it's essential to consider the pros and cons when deciding if it's an appropriate monetization method for your blog.

Sponsorships

Once you build a large audience, you can earn revenue through sponsorships.

With sponsorships, companies pay you to promote their products on your blog and/or social media pages. This is different from affiliate marketing because you don't earn a percentage of a sale but get paid a set rate for promoting a good—regardless of whether or not someone purchases said good.

This method is more difficult for new bloggers because most companies won't work with a blogger until they get a certain amount of website traffic or have a certain number of social media followers. However, if you meet the requirements, the earning potential with sponsored content can be massive.

Another factor to consider is that sponsored content can take some time to produce. When pricing a sponsored post, make sure to account for this time. If you wouldn't write a blog post for someone else for $25, don't write a sponsored blog post for $25.

Another thing to consider is that you will need to spend time on developing and cultivating positive, ongoing relationships with your sponsors. Like ad networks, there are programs you can join that help bloggers and influencers get paired with relevant sponsors.

Since sponsored content is one of the most expensive forms of advertising, even if you work with a program like this, you will still have to take time to go back and forth with the sponsor until the content is approved to publish.

The larger your traffic and following, the more potential you have to make money from sponsorships. However, it's important to avoid selling do-follow links on your blog. This is against Google's guidelines and can potentially put you at risk of a penalty that would hurt your website's traffic and SEO.

Also, you don't want to overdo it with your sponsored content. If everything you post is sponsored, you risk annoying your readers or followers. A general rule of thumb when it comes to sponsored content is to keep it under 30% of your content each month.

Membership

While the previously mentioned strategies are the most common ways to earn money from blogging, they aren't the only methods.

Another method is to set up a membership site. These sites use a system that collects an ongoing payment from members in exchange for exclusive access to members-only content. Setting this up on your site can be difficult. Another easier method is working with a third-party subscription service, such as Patreon.

The time commitment for subscription sites is commonly high. Your members will need some incentive to keep their membership, and that usually means you'll have ongoing work to produce content or resources for members.

However, if you're willing to put in the work, subscription sites can produce a steady, recurring revenue for content creators.

What monetization model is right for me?

There are numerous other ways to monetize your site that we won't expand on in this book. However, the above are the most common. Deciding which of the models to use can be difficult.

If you're just getting started or if your site has fewer than 30,000 monthly sessions or under 10,000 social media followers, the quickest ways to start monetizing your blog are display advertising and affiliate marketing. You can also create an e-commerce store from scratch, of course, but expect to spend a great deal of time and money on promoting your goods.

As your site grows, you can introduce more methods, such as selling your own goods, gaining sponsorships, and creating membership plans.

According to The Blog Millionaire Podcast's Blog Income Report Study, bloggers who made between $2,000 and $7,500 per month were, on average, making the most money from display advertising, followed by affiliate marketing.

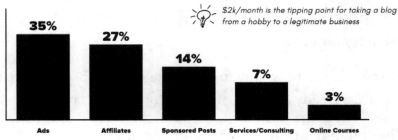

In the same study, bloggers who made between $7,500 and $25,000 per month were, on average, earning the majority of their income from affiliate marketing, display advertising, and sponsored posts.

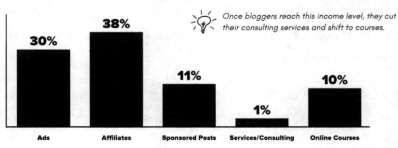

However, bloggers earning more than $25,000 per month were earning 80% of their income from products, more specifically, online courses.

DISTRIBUTION OF BLOGGING INCOME

BLOGGERS MAKING $25,000+/MONTH

80%

The wealthiest bloggers in the world make
80% of their income from online courses

12%

3%   **3%**   **0%**

Ads   Affiliates   Sponsored Posts   Services/Consulting   Online Courses

Credit: The Blog Millionaire

This data shows that producing your own goods has by far the largest earning potential. However, many beginner bloggers lack the following, authority, and resources to sell their own goods at the same level of blogging veterans.

Advertising and affiliate marketing are two methods that can result in quick wins, but they shouldn't be where you stop when it comes to making money as a blogger.

Creating content that sells

We know that businesses exist to serve the needs of the marketplace. For example, hot dog stands succeed when the following market forces are at work:

1. Customers desire hot dogs (demand)

2. Entrepreneurs create hot dogs (supply)

The market demand for blogs is outstanding. But what kind of blogs do people want to read?

There's a famous scene in the movie, *Gladiator*, when Antonius Proximo, a former slave turned slave owner, teaches the main character Maximus, played by Russell Crowe, how to win his freedom.

> *"I wasn't the best because I killed quickly. I was the best because the crowd loved me. Win the crowd. Win your freedom."*

Whether your blog inspires, informs, educates, or entertains, your content and its corresponding demand should be researched, validated, tested, analyzed, and improved.

How do you do this?

First and foremost, focus on your content. We don't mean to sound like a broken record, but it's essential for anyone wanting to become successful at blogging to understand that if you don't have content that people want to read, you have nothing.

In the last chapter, we talked about the importance of things like keyword research, backlink development, and conversion rate optimization. Having a deep understanding of each of these practices will help you become a more successful blogger.

Another key element to blog monetization is creating sales funnels. A sales funnel essentially represents the path a blog visitor must take to result in a conversion. Visually, a sales funnel looks something like this:

Your website traffic is at the top of the funnel. If you create content that brings people to your blog, you are on your way to making money as a blogger. The next step is getting you traffic to convert.

You do this by creating powerful calls-to-action (CTAs) in the form of text, graphics, ads, or pop-ups that encourage visitors to take the intended action.

Let's say you have a parenting blog, and you join the affiliate program of a company that produces cribs. The affiliate commission is 25%, and most of their cribs sell for around $200 each, which means you make around $50 per conversion.

So, your goal is to optimize your content in a way that encourages your blog visitors to purchase the cribs. One way to do this would be to write a review post where you personally review one of the cribs and talk about your own positive experiences with it. Within the post, you want to include several affiliate links to the product so visitors can easily click to view more information and make a purchase.

The next stage in the funnel is closing the sale. The downside to affiliate marketing is that bloggers lose control at this stage. They may spread awareness about a product, but it doesn't mean the reader will make a purchase.

However, if you're marketing your own goods, you can optimize the purchasing process to increase conversions. You can do this by implementing proven sales tactics like discounts and coupon codes, one-click shopping for returning customers, free shipping for physical products, an FAQ page, and chat bots.

The last stage of the funnel is to strengthen brand loyalty by offering special perks and discounts to returning customers to encourage them to return to your store. You can also implement a strategy called upselling, which is promoting goods that the customer will likely want in addition to the already purchased product.

Additional blogging business strategies

So far, we've talked about the common ways to make money from a single blog. Owning and operating one blog is by far the most popular way to blog.

Yet as entrepreneurs, investors, and the general public learn more about the financial benefits of blog ownership, the landscape is changing.

People are beginning to see blogs as the assets that they are. In many ways, owning a successful blog is much like owning a residential property. Essentially, you can think of your blog like online real estate.

Like with physical property management, successful bloggers are even realizing they can hire other people to manage and grow their blogging business while they continue to bring in a relatively passive income each month!

And the strategies can be replicated and used across additional sites. If you're willing to think big enough, you can turn your blog into an enterprise. But first, you have to learn how to scale your blog and start outsourcing work. We'll discuss exactly how to do this in the next chapter.

CHAPTER 5

From Good to Great: How to Scale Your Blogging Business

Before we begin this chapter, pause for a moment and ask yourself this question: Why do I want to start a blogging business?

This is most likely not the first time you've asked yourself this question. But in reflecting on your reason for starting a blogging business—your *purpose*—you're shifting your mindset to be ready to learn everything it takes to grow your business.

Mindset is an often overlooked, but essential, element to success as an entrepreneur. Many people start blogs because they're passionate about the subject matter or hope to make a supplemental income.

Some of the bloggers we spoke to when interviewing for this book said they never initially saw their blog as becoming a full-time business. They were shocked to find out how relatively easy it was to make money from blogging. And it was that realization that pushed them to move from a blogger mindset to an entrepreneur mentality.

But even those who do start blogging with the intention of building a successful business find themselves caught up in the details and logistics rather than prioritizing strategies for growth.

This is one reason why so many new businesses fail.

An entrepreneur may have a big idea for their business but then find themselves stuck in order management and customer service tasks. Suddenly, the excitement fades, and they realize they haven't built a business. They've just created another *job*.

How many bloggers have given up because they lost the passion for their blogs that they had in the beginning? Once it started to feel like a job, it was no longer exciting and meaningful.

You may even be feeling like you're nearing this place yourself, or maybe you've been there for a while.

Don't worry. There is a way out. And it starts with how you think.

From blogger to entrepreneur

One theme we've seen again and again in the blogging community over the years is one of sentimentality. So many bloggers treat their blogs as their babies.

You created the website. *You* wrote the first blog post. *You* attracted the first few readers. And unsurprisingly, *you* are unwilling to give up any control over the site to other people once it starts to grow.

First things first, as wonderful as your blog is, it is not your child. Again, *your blog is not your child.* (Repeat as often as necessary until it sinks in!)

If you want your site to ever be more than a hobby blog, you have to think about your blog as the business that it is.

This means knowing how to prioritize your time and when to let other people run parts of your business. If you're spending all of your time writing blog posts, sharing content on social media, and responding to emails, you're likely not dedicating enough time to strategizing how to grow your business.

While the fear of letting go of control is a major thing that holds bloggers back from success, another reason is financial. We've heard so many bloggers say things like, "I'd love to hire a virtual assistant to respond to all the reader emails I get, but I can't afford it."

Listen, we get it. It's hard to let go of any amount of income you're making from your site, especially initially when that number is relatively small. And, of course, you need an income to survive. But again, this is a mindset thing.

Don't think about it as paying someone else to respond to emails. Think about it as investing in your business. You get to find someone else capable of handling the tasks that are preventing you from investing your time and energy into strategic growth initiatives.

"But what if I like responding to emails from my readers?"

It's common for beginner and intermediate bloggers to hold on tightly to tasks because they say they actually enjoy them.

But if we dig even deeper into the heart of this statement, we often find it's actually because they don't *trust* anyone else to do the work as well as they can.

If you truly love doing a task that could be outsourced, set a specific amount of time each week to devote to it. For example, you can schedule four hours per week to write blog posts and outsource the rest of your content.

If you love engaging with your followers on social media, check in with them for 30 minutes each day, but don't spend every afternoon scrolling through Instagram.

As an entrepreneur who wants to grow a successful blogging business, your focus should always be on the work that's going to help your company make money. And that includes finding people to help you scale your business.

Building systems for success

So you're ready to start outsourcing, now what? Before you start hiring, the first thing you need to do is ensure you have the systems in place for your new hire to be successful.

Many bloggers lament that outsourcing doesn't work for them because they can't find anyone who's the right fit for the job. But the truth is, nearly anyone with some skill and interest in the work can be the right fit if the proper systems are in place that set them up for success.

You heard that right. *Nearly anyone.*

As a business owner, you'll stumble into issues with the wrong fit again and again if your expectation is for every new hire to read your mind and do things exactly like you would do them.

We made this mistake early on, too. We hired intelligent and hard-working VAs who struggled to fulfill expectations because those expectations and guidelines to help them achieve them weren't clearly defined.

So, we started documenting *everything*. Documentation can be a mind-numbing and tedious task for an entrepreneur, but once it's done, you never have to go back to doing that task again.

Create clear and detailed standard operating procedures (SOPs) that can guide your new hire through the work that you expect them to do. Create both a written document as well as a step-by-step video tutorials that walk them through the tasks.

Bonus: We've got a few FREE SOPs just for you! Head over to EinsteinBlogging.com to get them.

You can always refine your SOPs as you go or even ask your new hire to help refine them once they get familiar with the job. The important thing is that they have something to work off of as soon as they start working with you.

Another crucial document to create before you hire someone is a job description. In the description, list the day-to-day responsibilities and expectations of the position. This should be something both you and the new hire can reference frequently to determine if they're fulfilling the expectations of the role.

To create this description, you first need to ask yourself what exactly you are looking for. Dig deeper than simply, "I want someone to write blog posts" or "I want someone to manage my social media accounts."

Instead ask questions like:

- Will they need to keep my tone/voice?

- Do they need experience using the tools my business uses?

- Do they need to have expert knowledge of topics in my niche?

- Should they have experience writing and/or managing their own blog?

- Are they comfortable working in a fast-paced, startup environment?

By having a clear picture of your ideal hire, you set yourself up to attract and hire the right person from the beginning.

Once you determine who your ideal candidate is, the next step is to make sure they'll have everything they need before you bring them onboard. If you expect them to use your project management system, you have a responsibility to provide them with the resources that allow them to learn how to use that system.

This may seem like a lot of upfront work, but think about the amount of time potentially wasted by hiring and firing the wrong people because you didn't invest time in setting your new hires up for success.

The sooner you start documenting and systematizing your work and setting clear role descriptions and expectations, the sooner you can hire people to successfully help you manage your business.

Outsourcing like a pro

Okay, so you have your processes documented and have answered the above questions about what you're looking for in a prospective employee. Now what?

Once you have a job description document, you can add a hiring page to your website and share that with your readers and social media followers. You can also share your hiring page in online forums and free job boards.

Make sure that you have a plan in place for how to handle the submissions. For most roles, you'll want to schedule an interview. A phone or video call is generally best, but email works in some cases.

A few things you'll definitely want to ask for are:

- A portfolio or samples of their work, if applicable

- References and/or a letter of recommendation

- Their preferred rates and hours

- For some roles, like writing or editing, it's good practice to have them do a short writing or editing test so you can evaluate their work

The above bullets will help you vet the skill level of the prospect, but it's also important to ask questions that will help you understand if they're a good fit for your business.

When we are vetting potential employees, we always look for the three Cs: competence, chemistry, and character.

- Is this person **competent** enough to fulfill the role?

- Do I have **chemistry** with this person? Do we get along? Is communication productive and effective?

- Are they a good **character** fit? Do they have a growth mindset? Do they face their fears? How honest are they with themselves and others?

Lastly, we look for a good sense of humor. A sense of humor is a sign of pattern recognition, so it can help you score someone's IQ. And someone with a sense of humor is generally just enjoyable to be around!

You can ask specific questions in the interview to get a stronger sense of competence, chemistry, and character.

These can be questions or leading statements, such as:

- What are three words your closest friends would use to describe you?

- Describe a time you faced a challenging situation at work and how you overcame it.

- Tell me about a time that you improved on an established way of doing something.

- Tell me about a time you had a particularly heavy course load. How did you manage your time?

- What goals have you set for yourself for this year/the next few years? How do you stay on track to meet your goals?

Another great way to pre-vet a potential employee is by sourcing word-of-mouth recommendations from trusted sources. You can reach out to other bloggers to see if they have any freelancer or virtual assistant recommendations.

If you don't know any other bloggers, join an online blogging community, like a Facebook group, and search for recommendations there. Other bloggers will be able to give you specific information on why they liked a certain contractor as well as answer any questions you have about the person or the type of work they do.

How to set your new hire up for success

Hiring your first employee, even if it's just outsourcing a couple of blog posts each month, is a huge accomplishment! It means that you've overcome the need to control everything about your business and put trust into another individual to help your website succeed.

Before you begin working with this new person, it's essential that you set them up for success. If you've already written the job description and have the appropriate SOPs in place, you're more than halfway there. But there are a few other things to think about.

1. *Create a training plan*

If you want to build a successful working relationship with a new employee, you need to convey the message that you and your business are organized and running a tight ship. Since you are likely working with a limited budget, now is not the time to throw a new employee into the deep end and see if they can swim.

Setting them up for success from the get-go will save you time, money, and headaches in the long run. You can start off on the right track by creating a training plan.

Before your employee starts, create a training plan for the first week. In the training, make sure you cover things like:

- An overview of you, your company, and your goals

- Tips for working well with you and any other team members, if applicable

- What kind of communication you expect from them and how often

- The approval process for their work

- How to find all the information they'll need to do their job

- Confidentiality policies

Prepare as much information as possible before the employee's first day and plan to go through the training with them more thoroughly during the first week.

You'll also want to make sure that all logistics are ready in advance, such as an email address or login credentials for software and websites the employee will need to use.

2. *Check in regularly*

Employees can sometimes take up to six months to get fully comfortable with a new role. Make sure you're checking in frequently with your new hire. If you're working with someone from another country, it's especially important to make sure there are no miscommunication issues.

After the first month or so, plan to meet virtually with your new hire to see how things are going. Ask questions like:

- Did your job turn out to be as you expected it would be when you were being hired?

- What areas would you like additional training or help with?

- Are you clear on what's expected of you and how you're doing against those expectations?

- How's your workload?

- Are there any obstacles that make doing your job more difficult?

Consistent communication, especially in the beginning, will relieve you of many common issues new entrepreneurs have when hiring their first employees.

3. Be consistent

If you're properly prepared before hiring your first employee, consistency will be easier than if you hire on impulse.

It's common for things to change quickly in the world of blogging, but be wary of making massive changes to your new employee's job role. It's one thing to say, "Hey, you're doing a great job of blog writing, can you also write three social media posts to go along with each blog?" but it's another thing entirely to say, "You're great at writing blogs, can you start working on this data entry project as well?"

Remember, just because your new employee kicks ass at one thing doesn't mean they are willing or able to do all the work that you don't want to do. If you hired them for specific skill sets, stick to giving them work in line with those skills as much as possible.

Also, be consistent with anything you communicated to them during the hiring process. Did you promise a winter bonus if they achieved a certain goal? Make sure you stick to your promises to ensure a positive relationship with your new hire.

Growing beyond your first employee

Remember, the goal of outsourcing work is to give you, the business owner, more time to focus on growing your business.

However, many blog owners as they scale begin to struggle with what to focus on next. Just like in the beginning stages of starting a blog, you may feel overwhelmed at the many possibilities and directions you can go next.

This is where you'll come back to that question we asked in the beginning of this chapter, "Why do I want to start a blogging business?"

Write your answer to this question somewhere you can see it every day, so you're constantly reminded of your purpose.

If your purpose is to make a lot of money, your focus should always be on how to make a lot of money. If it's to help people, then focus your time and energy on helping others. Where your purpose lies, that is the direction your attention should always go.

While staying mindful of your purpose will help you focus and stay on track with your goals, it's extremely likely that you'll still feel unsure or overwhelmed at times. That's the nature of growth, and it's perfectly normal.

Here are a few tips to help you successfully scale your business.

1. Learn from what others are doing

If you're not already following bloggers who are where you want to be, start doing that now. Luckily, there are a ton of successful bloggers who have been in your shoes, and many openly share the challenges they've faced and how they overcame them.

Look for people who offer consultations or online groups to further explore what's worked for other people. Online forums are a terrific place to ask questions and see what's working well for other bloggers.

One-on-one consultations and mastermind groups can also be beneficial to help you learn where to focus your attention next and what mistakes to avoid. Sharing your triumphs and challenges with others also helps you hold yourself accountable and reduces the stress of not accomplishing your goals as quickly as you may have planned.

2. *Define your business values—and stick with them*

It's important early on to determine what your business values are and stick to those values. So much will change as your business grows, but your values are the one thing that should stay consistent.

For example, perhaps a value is that you always offer exceptional customer service, no matter what. As things speed up, you notice you have less time to respond to customer complaints. If you choose to ignore your value by just not responding as promptly, your business will suffer the consequences.

If you're too busy to respond to every individual customer complaint, then you need to think about how you can adjust your workload to make time for that priority, improve your business model to reduce the number of complaints, or hire someone else to respond.

Identifying and sticking to your business values will help you remember what to focus on when things start to move fast.

3. Focus on quality over quantity

Once your blog starts bringing in a decent amount of revenue per month, and you begin to outsource some of your work, you'll likely start to focus more on how to get the most from what you're spending.

Maybe you hired someone to write blog posts for $75 per article, but later you found someone else who can do it for $50. Being savvy with your finances is crucial for the success of your business, but you should draw the line when it comes to quality.

In the world of blogging, quality content is key. You can always find someone who will do work for less, and sometimes you'll find extremely talented people willing to work within a small budget.

But don't be so focused on saving money that you let the quality of what your business is outputting suffer drastically.

When it comes to how much you do versus how well you do it, you'll always find more success with the latter approach.

4. Stay on top of trends and consider potential future outcomes

You don't need to be able to predict the future to be a successful entrepreneur, but staying aware of potential changes to your business and industry will help you stay prepared and adapt as needed.

Make sure that you've set up your analytics early on so you can monitor them for any changes and patterns in seasonality. You should also keep a close eye on your revenue and things that can impact it, such as changes to things like affiliate commission structures and advertising rates.

Looking into the future can also help set you up for success as you prepare your content to peak at exactly the right time.

You can use tools, like Google Trends, to see when specific topics are most popular and create content around that topic three or more months in advance.

For example, if you want to create several blog posts for Easter, don't wait until March to start writing those articles. Have the Easter blog posts ready by January and make a plan on how to promote them via social media and your email list early on.

5. *Outsource first what drains most*

In the blogging world, the beginning is the hardest part. Once you have the inertia, you'll start to be grateful you put in the work. But up front, it's tough to sustain and gain momentum—especially with your energy levels.

So, we suggest hiring out the work that drains the most precious resource you have, and one that aligns the most with persistence (see Chapter 2)... that is your energy.

Growth from the inside out

Building systems and hiring outside help can sound intimidating for many new bloggers—or even for pro bloggers who are used to handling it all on their own. However, getting comfortable with these things will not only grow your website, but also result in growth for you as an entrepreneur as well.

You may be someone who loves coming up with ideas and testing the ideas you come up with to see how they work. But creating systems and processes? Collaborating with other people to turn your vision into reality? These things may sound scary at first, but professional growth often requires personal growth as well.

You have to be able to do hard things and make difficult decisions to achieve the ultimate freedom and purpose you're looking for with your blogging business. And the best part is, while they seem like mountains from far away, up close they are only small hills. Once you climb them and get to the other side, you can look back and laugh at how challenging they appeared.

Now you know the steps required to scale your business. In the next chapter, we'll explore the 10 lessons you need to know to blog smarter, not harder.

CHAPTER 6

How to Blog Smarter, Not Harder

W e live in an era where we can have whatever we want delivered to our doorstep in a matter of hours. Collectively, we are programming humanity to expect instant gratification.

When it comes to blogging, many people entering the business have similar expectations. Surely, they think, there are a few hacks that will make me rich within months, right?

This book is full of tips, tricks, and insider secrets that can make you a lot of money. But it would be a huge misconception to believe that you'll turn into a millionaire overnight. If any form of entrepreneurship were that easy, everyone would be doing it.

Your blog is your business. And any business owner will tell you that entrepreneurship takes hard work, persistence, and risk. You have to be willing to win *and lose.*

"A person who never made a mistake never tried anything new." - Albert Einstein

It's in our greatest failures and mistakes as business owners that we learn the most transformative lessons.

At Wander Media, we made plenty of mistakes when we started. For example, we closed on the purchase of an Amazon Affiliates website the **same day** that Amazon updated their affiliate commission structure for the website's niche from 8% to 3%. The website's value tanked immediately, and we lost a lot of money as a result.

Is it fun making mistakes? Nope. Are the lessons learned invaluable? Yep!

As a blogger, you will have an opportunity to learn so many essential lessons on your own. Hands-on experience will teach you more than anything you'll get from any book(including this one!).

But from our own failures and mistakes and those of other successful bloggers we interviewed, we've compiled a list of the top 10 lessons every blogger needs to learn to blog smarter, not harder.

Lesson #1: You won't get far if you stay inside your comfort zone.

The main reason that bloggers don't pursue full-time entrepreneurship is fear.

Everyone experiences fear. Even the biggest thrill-seekers feel fear. The difference between someone who's willing to jump out of an airplane or quit their full-time job to be an entrepreneur and someone who isn't is that the thrill-seeker channels their fear into actionable energy.

"Fear fear less"

The blogger who grows the most is the one with the most courage, which we define as the ability to feel and face your fears. It's not *being unafraid* of challenges that matters. It's the courage to persist.

"Success is not final, failure is not fatal: it is the courage to continue that counts." - Winston Churchill

Instead of dwelling on the negative what-ifs, these people focus on positive opportunities, and then they act on them. They're energized by the chance to do something different and new. They're excited about what's in store.

The more we become content with stability, the harder it becomes to live outside of our comfort zones. And with so much uncertainty in the world around us, that's understandable. It's nice to be comfortable.

But here's the hard truth: If you prioritize your comfort over entrepreneurship, you will not make it. You have to take risks. You have to commit to doing things that scare you.

Don't worry. You CAN do it. But…

Lesson #2: You can't do it all on your own.

So many bloggers spend unnecessary time stressing out about all the things that they *can't* do.

- "I get so many emails every day, and I don't have enough time to respond to them. It's overwhelming!"

- "I just don't have enough time to write blog posts four times per week and send weekly emails and manage my social media pages!"

- "I want to create an offer for my website, but I don't know how to design!"

When beginner bloggers run into these problems, their instinct is to devote an inordinate amount of time on learning how to do all the things on their own. For example, they may invest hundreds and thousands of dollars into courses to learn skills that cost $6 an hour to hire if you know where to go.

If they do invest in help, it's usually a system or tool that will help them streamline some of the work. But they're still doing the work and still feeling overwhelmed by it.

One of the most important things to learn is this: You can't do it all. There is no way you can turn your blog into a successful business without being willing to give up some control and hire outside help.

Building a successful blogging business means thinking of it as a business, not as a hobby. If you're going to invest any money into your blog, invest it in the people who can help you.

Why spend four hours a day responding to emails when you can spend that time on things that will help your business grow?

This is where a lot of bloggers get stuck. Their blog is their baby. And they're scared to step outside of their comfort zone and put any part of the process in someone else's hands. But you can't grow as long as you stay stuck inside a fear-based mindset.

Accept that you can't do it all on your own. Then find people who can help.

Lesson #3: One mistake is not the end of the world.

Have you ever been in a toxic work environment? The type of place where everyone walks on eggshells, afraid that if they make just one mistake everything will completely blow up?

Unfortunately, this type of environment is far too common. And it's one reason so many people decide to leave the 9 to 5 life to start their own business.

If you come from this sort of toxic environment or are prone to placing extremely high expectations on yourself, you can accidentally bring this same toxicity to your business.

You have to allow room for imperfections in your blogging business. Mistakes are inevitable. You will make them. The people you hire will make them. No matter how ideal your systems, processes, and people are, *mistakes will still happen.*

It can be difficult to let go of the expectations you learned to accept from toxic environments. But it's crucial that you're conscious about not accepting those types of unrealistic expectations when it comes to your business.

Of course, this doesn't mean not setting high standards or big goals. It simply means understanding that mistakes happen, but one mistake doesn't define you as a business owner.

Keep going.

Lesson #4: Think big but plan small.

Jas Bagniewski, co-founder of Eve Sleep said, "Don't get distracted. Never tell yourself that you need to be the biggest brand in the whole world. Start by working on what you need at the present moment and then what you need to do tomorrow. So, set yourself manageable targets."

Most entrepreneurs would beg to differ with Bagniewski's advice. Why? Entrepreneurs are dreamers.

Do you ever feel like you have a million big ideas for your business but aren't sure exactly how to turn all of them into reality? Of course, you do.

The ability to dream big is a valuable skill. But successful entrepreneurs know that dreaming isn't enough. When it comes to actually accomplishing goals, take Bagniewski's advice and plan small.

Focus on what you can do today, tomorrow, this week, and this month. It's OK to say, "I want to own a six-figure business in one year." But the dream alone won't make it happen.

Setting S.M.A.R.T. goals, or goals that are specific, measurable, achievable, results-focused and time-bound, will help you plan actionable tasks that will allow you to reach your big picture goals faster.

For example, if your big goal is to make $5,000 per month from your blog by the end of the year, your S.M.A.R.T. goals could be:

- Increase website traffic by publishing five keyword-focused blog posts per week until the end of the year.

- Grow my email list by creating, publishing, and promoting a free e-book on my website and social media pages by August 1.

- Join an advertising network once my website traffic reaches 10,000 sessions per month.

All of these separate S.M.A.R.T. goals are connected because they have one thing in common—making more money from your blog. And now you have specific steps with deadlines to take that will help you meet your big picture goals.

Lesson #5: Don't follow someone else's path and expect the same results.

Many bloggers and entrepreneurs hold the belief that if they can just learn what worked for someone else, it will work for them.

There is some truth to this belief. It's much easier to grow from a strong foundation than it is to try to build that foundation from scratch.

If you want to grow a garden, you can't just go outside with some seeds in your pocket and expect a healthy garden to miraculously bloom. You're much more likely to successfully grow your garden if you research, buy the right tools, gain some gardening experience, and follow advice from expert gardeners.

One great thing about blogging is that, like gardening, there are many people out there doing it successfully and sharing their tips and resources. These tips and resources make it so much easier to get started.

It's not a mistake to take advice from others. But it is a mistake to expect the exact same results.

This is something we've learned from owning more than ten blogs. What works for one blog doesn't always work for another.

To truly understand what *does* work, you have to understand your blog, your niche, your audience, and your goals. These things will be different for different people and different blogs.

Even the most tried and true methods may need to be modified to work for your business. Clutching on to a system that isn't working for you, just because it worked for someone else, is only going to lead to failure.

This leads us to the next lesson...

Lesson #6: Start, Stop, Continue.

Do you ever feel like you worked extremely hard all week, but by the weekend you find yourself asking, What did I actually accomplish?

Every blogger reaches the stage of their blogging business when it feels like there is always so much going on, but they're not sure what is actually working.

Maybe you've hired a couple of writers or a virtual assistant. You're looking at the first month's invoice and asking yourself, "Is it worth it? Are these people really bringing value to my blogging business?"

To successfully manage a growing business, you need systems in place that help you evaluate your own performance and the performances of others.

This is where the Start, Stop, Continue exercise comes to play. Start, Stop, Continue is a tested method to increase productivity and get more value out of the various tasks you're working on.

The Start, Stop, Continue format focuses on:

- Start: New ideas and things that you and your team should start doing

- Stop: Things that are not working

- Continue: Things that are working

We practice the Start, Stop, Continue exercise on a monthly basis. Specifically, we look at:

- What our team accomplished during the last month

- What worked and what didn't

- What needs to change

- How we will implement new ideas.

Here's an example of what Start, Stop, Continue may look like in a blogging business:

- Start:

  - Keyword research for holiday-focused blog posts

  - New email sequence promoting free offer

- Stop:

  - Posting polls to Instagram stories (little engagement)

  - Advertising free offer on Facebook (no downloads)

- Continue:

  - Publishing ten affiliate-focused blog posts per month

  - Sponsorship campaign on Instagram

The Start, Stop, Continue method will help you eliminate non-productive tasks, ideate and implement new possibilities, and more effectively manage your time and the time of your team members.

Lesson #7: Invest in your business and yourself.

One of the biggest mistakes bloggers-turned-business owners make is not investing enough money made from their blog back into their business.

They view their blog revenue as an extra source of income to live off of. This is a dangerous mindset because if you're hoarding the majority of your blogging income, you have less to invest in growing your business.

Instead, set yourself a base salary and invest the rest of your revenue into growing your business. Your base salary should be just enough to cover basic expenses. You can set a S.M.A.R.T. goal to re-evaluate your base salary after a set amount of time.

Until then, resist the urge to increase your salary as your business grows. Instead, come up with a plan for how to invest this additional income into your business.

Here's an example: Let's say your blog is making $4,000 per month, and you're ready to leave your job to pursue blogging full-time. You set your base salary to $3,000 per month, which is less than you were making in your full-time job, but enough to get by for at least one year.

Once you've set S.M.A.R.T. goals for growth, you can start to project your business growth over the next year. And you can plan how to invest your revenue as it grows.

Here's an example:

- Once my blog makes $5,000 per month, I'll spend $1,000 in outsourced blog content per month.

- Once my blog makes $6,000 per month, I'll hire a full-time virtual assistant to manage my social media accounts,

- Once my blog makes $10,000 per month, I'll increase my monthly salary to $4,000.

If you don't think in terms of investing your revenue back into your business, it likely means you're thinking of your blog as a job, not as a business.

And this brings us to the next lesson...

Lesson #8: Outsource, outsource, outsource.

We didn't turn Wander Media into a six-figure blogging business by having two people do all the work.

Today, the Wander Media team is made up of 7+ full-time workers and numerous freelancers. We use Slack to communicate quickly and efficiently with all of our team members. As the owners, we focus on managing our team members although we've even outsourced a lot of that at this point and, more importantly, growing our business.

How do we do this?

Outsource, outsource, outsource.

In his book, *The E-Myth Revisited: Why Most Small Businesses Don't Work and What to Do About It*, author Michael E. Gerber writes that one of the keys to a successful business model is that it's able to be operated by people with the lowest possible level of skill.

Gerber references the success of McDonald's. The company's growth is often attributed to its seamless processes that have since been replicated by fast food chains around the world.

The reason McDonald's works is because nearly anyone can be trained to successfully follow its processes.

This doesn't mean that the employees lack skill or intelligence. What it means is that the system is so strong, not even the employee with the lowest level of skill could destroy it.

Of course, every business owner wants to hire competent employees. Please don't mistake this lesson as telling you to do otherwise. But if you want a successful business, you need to set up processes that even those with little skill or knowledge can follow.

At Wander Media, we have a knowledge base full of SOPs (standard operating procedures) for nearly every task that our team members work on. If we want to implement a new task, we create a new SOP and add it to the knowledge base.

It's boring and tedious work to set up systems unless you're just the type of person who enjoys these things. But do you know what it allows you to do in the long term?

Outsource, outsource, outsource.

Lesson #9: Believe in your content.

Words like "meaningful" and "authentic" are frequently overused in the world of blogging. When you view your blog like a business, you can't be too attached to making sure every detail passes the "is this a true, authentic representation of everything I stand for?" inspection. Essentially, *you've got to be okay with letting some of that go.*

But if you eliminate any meaning or purpose from your business, it quickly becomes just as fulfilling as the job you left to pursue it. (which means, not fulfilling at all!)

Your blog is a resource that can provide you a place to work out the pursuit of meaning. Writing about a topic and becoming an authority and thought leader on that topic can give you true purpose and fulfillment.

Communicating with billions of people has a way of calling bullshit on your authenticity. If you don't care about what you're saying, *you'll find out quickly*. And if you don't, you'll likely hear it in feedback from other people.

But if you do believe in the content you're creating, you'll discover a long-term, sustainable way to market something that brings you joy, fulfillment, and money.

Lesson #10: Believe in yourself.

The first and last lessons in this chapter are the most important because they tackle what is perhaps the most difficult challenge entrepreneurs face: doubt.

You cannot prevent doubt from creeping in at the most inopportune moments:

- When you face a massive setback, there's doubt.

- When you compare yourself to someone else, there's doubt.

- When you're not sure if you'll be able to pay your bills this month, there's doubt.

Again and again, doubt pops up to tell you to go back to your comfort zone. Go back to that place of safety and security.

If you want to be successful, you have to be able to look doubt in the face and say, "Fuck off, doubt."

There are highs and lows when it comes to building a blogging business. But if you don't believe that you can do it and if you allow doubt to replace your drive to succeed, you won't make it.

If you find yourself wallowing in doubt, focus on projects that energize you. If you're someone who loves to learn, then read a new book or take a new course. If you need to talk through what you're going through, call up a friend or search for an accountability group. Take some time away from what's dragging you down to refocus and remember why you started this in the first place.

At the end of the day, no matter how much you know and how much work you do, your business won't thrive if you don't believe in it and if you don't believe in *you*.

We'll leave you with this quote from speaker and author Mark Hanson:

"Don't wait until everything is just right. It will never be perfect. There will always be challenges, obstacles, and less than perfect conditions. So what? Get started now. With each step you take, you will grow stronger and stronger, more and more skilled, more and more self-confident, and more and more successful."

CHAPTER 7

Insider Secrets From Successful Bloggers

If you've made it this far in the book, it's safe to assume that you are committed to growing a successful blogging business. Your willingness to make this commitment is a big deal, so first and foremost, congratulations!

There is so much we can learn from the successes—*and failures*—of others. In the next few chapters, you'll find case studies for three successful bloggers, each making *six-figures or more* from their blogging business.

Within this chapter, we've broken down some of the most important lessons and insider secrets—straight from the mouths of some of the most successful bloggers.

What is success in blogging?

Before we dive into the insider secrets from successful bloggers, it's important to define what we mean by the word "success." Success may look different for you, depending on what you are hoping to achieve with your business. For every blogger, success has its own unique meaning.

Remember the "why" behind your blogging journey that you determined way back in Chapter 1? This should help you determine what success in blogging looks like for you.

Take a moment to remind yourself of your why, then think about what success looks like for you. Success could be:

- Growing a six-figure (or more) business

- Making a difference in your niche or community

- Having the flexibility to travel the world

- Connecting with like-minded people

- Gaining millions of followers on social media

Whatever your reason may be, it's essential to have a clear understanding of how you define success.

1. *The most successful bloggers focus on blog age, posting frequency, and social media, according to **Darren Rowse of Pro Blogger.***

Pro Blogger, founded by Darren Rowse in 2004, is one of the earliest and biggest resources specifically for bloggers. So, it's not surprising that Rowse is full of expert advice for bloggers.

In the book, *ProBlogger: Secrets for Blogging Your Way to a Six-Figure Income,* authored by Rowse and Chris Garrett, the authors state:

"When we looked at the top blogs and bloggers around us, we found they had certain elements in common between them, regardless of niche, monetization method, and motivation. In particular, age, posting frequency, and social media all seem to focus heavily on their success."

They go on to explain that the average age of most successful blogs is 33.8 months. While Pro Blogger was originally published back in 2008, this is something that has remained constant over time. Search engines factor in website age when determining ranking. While it is possible to grow a new blog fast, in nearly all circumstances, patience is a virtue. Growing your blog takes time.

"The first lesson to take away is that blogging is a long-term thing, but it is possible to have success much faster—with luck and a lot of hard work," Rowse says.

One way to do this is to post frequently. Many successful bloggers post more often than others, especially in the initial stages of their blog growth. Search engines like to see fresh content. However, it's not enough to just have content, you'll need to have *high quality content.*

Most of the top blogs are written by multiple authors. Finding or hiring guest writers will make it much easier to increase your posting frequency. Most successful bloggers post about once per day, mixing their own posts with articles from guest writers.

Active social media pages also help boost your blog readership, Rowse says.

"The aim is maintain a good ratio between conversation, sharing good content from third parties (including links that you find and re-sharing what your network sends you), and posting your own links."

2. *The most successful bloggers focus on long-term, sustainable traffic, according to* **Ben Huber of Dollar Sprout.**

It may sound fun to focus your blogging on things that are currently trending—which is all well and fine, as it does tend to get the most traction on social media. However, unless you already have a large and engaged audience on social media, you're less likely to see the results you want from that type of content.

"I think the most relevant tactic a blogger can employ is learning the synergies between content creation and marketing. Certain types of content are easy to market, certain types of content are not," said Ben.

"If you're not developing content with search intent in mind, and you're not a professional media buyer, you're down to a single avenue for acquiring traffic—organic social."

In many ways, Ben explains, organic social is a dying breed. With algorithms that aren't as generous as they once were (on the most popular social media platforms), ad revenue considerations as they are, and engagement-based timeline surfacing on pretty much every feed, it's extremely difficult to consistently hit enough home runs on social to gain considerable traffic.

"We realized that by researching moderately popular long tail keywords on platforms like Pinterest and Google, we were able to go after frequently searched terms that weren't as beat to death, and grow our audience ad revenue that way," he said.

What's more, an article that performs well on social, say Pinterest, also tends to perform well in search and vice versa. So, if you find a keyword that applies to both, it's often a homerun in terms of getting long-term, sustainable traffic.

3. *The most successful bloggers learn how to buy and flip websites, according to* **Richard Patey of RichardPatey.com.**

Richard Patey is an expert in website flipping and sales funnels. He has built and sold his own six-figure website, and he offers advice for bloggers looking to do the same on his website, RichardPatey.com.

If you're brand new to blogging, website flipping may not be right for you. But if you already have the skillset to operate and grow a blog, it's an excellent way to make more money from blogging.

Richard's website flipping model focuses on doubling a website's income and asset value in a short period of time. He suggests the below strategies to double a site's value:

- Doubling conversion rate on an under-optimized site if you are a CRO master

- Improving Domain Authority by being able to redirect powerful links

- Optimizing ad monetization or swapping from one ad network to another

- Content pruning: reducing keyword cannibalization or improving crawlability by reducing index bloat

- Doubling opt-in rates if you are a sales funnel expert

- Doubling average order value on digital products by adding upsell funnels

Website flipping is a bit more advanced than beginner blogging and can require a significant financial investment. So make sure you've done your research before buying and flipping a blog. You can search for blogs for sale on sites, such as Empire Flippers and Flippa (We've personally had good experiences buying blogs from both of these sites).

Of course, the tried and true blogging methods also work when flipping websites although it may take some time to sow the fruits of your labor.

Richard notes, "You can also double a website's value by simply investing in new top quality content, but the results from that take longer to materialise and that's an additional expense that you need to budget for... However it's an approach I personally like to deploy when picking up non-revenue generating micro-acquisitions based on traffic value."

4. *The most successful bloggers focus on content, not followers, according to **Alex and Lauren of Create + Go**.*

Alex and Lauren from Create + Go built two six-figure blogs and went from broke to $100,000 per month in under three years. In that time, they also grew each of their social media pages to tens of thousands of followers.

But in a blog post, Lauren said that their success was in focusing on content, NOT followers.

"Everyone always gets so worked up over follower counts. I get it. It's a social proof thing. It's a popularity contest," writes Lauren. "I get it. Sometimes you don't get taken seriously if you don't have a certain amount of followers. They are important for these reasons. You have to be careful though. Followers aren't always a sign of success."

The reason? Simply acquiring followers may make you appear like an authority from the outside looking in, but there is a clear difference between someone with a large amount of followers and someone with authority online: engagement.

Sure, you can try to game the system and use spammy methods to buy followers and increase your follower count. But you'll have terrible engagement rates, and the people following you aren't likely to visit your website or convert.

Lauren says, "The content that you produce matters infinitely more than followers do when it comes to actually driving traffic to your blog. Followers are useless if they aren't engaging with your content anyway."

"The content that you produce matters infinitely more than followers do when it comes to actually driving traffic to your blog."

5. *The most successful bloggers prioritize building their email list, according to* **Tracie Fobes of TracieFobes.com.**

Many new bloggers are so focused on getting traffic to their website and growing their social media presence that they completely neglect their email list.

When we talk to bloggers who are selling their websites and ask about an email list, we usually get a response that goes something like this:

"Yeah, I put a sign-up form on my blog, but I haven't really done much with email."

Neglecting email marketing is a massive-missed opportunity. Blogging coach Tracie Fobes notes the importance of email marketing on her website:

"Social media and organic search are great, but those platforms aren't always in our control. One small tweak to the algorithm and you can lose ranking and the ability for your readers to see what you share. They decide who can see what," Tracie says. "Those changes can affect you negatively. One change and your pageviews can tank. You need to ensure you are always getting the traffic and clicks you need to sustain and grow your income."

In the ever-evolving world of blogging, email is one outreach method that has remained constant over time. And it doesn't appear to be going anywhere soon. Make sure that you are focusing on email as much as other distribution channels.

"Your list is always there no matter what changes you see happening online. It will never go away," says Tracie. "If someone tells you email is dead, they'd be wrong. Email works."

6. *The most successful bloggers follow their passions... maybe, according to **author and blogger Chris Guillebeau.***

Many young people today grew up hearing the wise advice to "follow your dreams" and "pursue your passions." We're not being contemptuous. Following your passions is, in fact, sage advice.

But as a business owner, you have to be able to look at your business objectively and consider how it truly brings value to your readers and customers.

In his bestselling book, *The $100 Startup*, Chris Guillebeau writes:

"Building a business around a passion can be a great fit for many people, but not everyone. In the rush to pursue a passion, a number of things get left out. First, you can't just pursue any passion. There are plenty of things you may be passionate about that no one will pay you for... You must focus continually on how your project can help other people, and why they'll care about what you're offering in the first place."

For example, if you love to garden, you may want to start a gardening blog. You talk about your garden and post pictures of your plants, but no one is paying attention. Why not? Because sharing your passion for gardening is not offering something of value to your reader.

Rather, you can share gardening advice, tutorials, and guides that educate your readers about the joys of gardening.

"The missing piece is that you usually don't get paid for your hobby itself; you get paid for helping other people pursue the hobby or for something indirectly related to it," Chris writes. "I began my career by sharing stories about a quest to visit every country in the world, but I don't get paid for that. I have to create value in my business the same way anyone else does. Without real value, I wouldn't get paid, and the travel would just be a hobby (albeit a passionate one)."

7. *The most successful bloggers think outside the box... within their limits, according to* **Brian Halligan and Dharmesh Shah of HubSpot.**

The best way to stand out as a blogger and attract website visitors is to focus your content on a topic or topics that are in high demand but have low competition. The higher the competition, the higher the value of what you offer needs to be.

If you want to start a blog that's focused on advice for new bloggers, you'll be competing with a lot of experienced and successful bloggers. So the question becomes: How can I rethink what I have to offer in a way that's still valuable, yet different from my competition?

In their book, *Inbound Marketing: Attract, Engage, and Delight Customers Online*, HubSpot co-founders Brian Halligan and Dharmesh Shah write:

"If you are not the world's best within your market, redefine your market more narrowly before one of your competitors takes that position."

In the book, the authors give a fictitious example of a monkey wrench manufacturer in San Diego that sells mainly to plumbers in southern California. The manufacturer wants to expand beyond the region, but competition in other regions is fierce.

Rather than try to compete with these manufacturers, the company pivots. It focuses instead on monkey wrenches for left-handed plumbers. Since there are more left-handed plumbers worldwide than total plumbers in southern California, the business explodes and becomes known as the top manufacturer of left-handed monkey wrenches.

Thinking outside the box doesn't have to mean doing something big and brand new. Sometimes it simply means looking at what you're already doing and asking: How can I do this differently and better?

The HubSpout founders conclude, "If you cannot rethink your boundaries to get yourself a broad untapped market the way Apple did with the iPod, then you should narrow your boundaries within your existing market and become the world's best within those boundaries."

The road to success starts with you

Becoming a blogger is easy. All you have to do is start a blog. On the other hand, becoming a successful blogger takes effort, patience, and determination. It also means learning from others and applying their wisdom as you pave your own unique path.

In the next three chapters, we had the privilege of interviewing and highlighting three successful bloggers. Each blogger shares their own challenges and successes as well as the most important lessons they've learned along the way.

We know you will be as inspired and motivated by these entrepreneurs as we are.

CHAPTER 8

How Tracie Fobes Turned Her Personal Finance Blog Into a Six-Figure Online Business

Tracie Fobes started her first blog in January 2009 with a single mission: to help families learn how to manage their money and get out of debt.

"I had no idea what a blog even was!" Tracie said. "I had been sharing deals in a private forum, and a friend told me to do a blog. I started putting them there and began sharing what we were doing to get out of debt. I had no clue about making money or turning it into a business."

Tracie knew that to turn her blog into a profitable business, she would need to develop some goals. So, she sat down and listed out her goals for the next five years:

- Year 1: At least 1,000 visits a month and $100 in monthly income.

- Year 3: At least 3,000 visits a month and $300 in monthly income.

- Year 5: At least 5,000 visits a month and $500 in monthly income.

In August 2009, Tracie received her first check for $65 from affiliate posts. That was the moment she realized the potential to turn her hobby blog into a full-time business.

From there, Tracie dove deep into the world of blogging. She learned everything she could about how to make money as a blogger. And before she knew it, she had exceeded her five-year goal in the first year.

Within her first two years of blogging, Tracie was able to pay off more than $35,000 in debt from the income she was making from her site. And nearly a decade later, Tracie was able to sell her blog, The Penny Pinchin' Mom, for six-figures.

Today, Tracie advises and inspires hundreds of bloggers using her years of experience. She's living the life beginner bloggers dream of living. But, she says, it didn't happen overnight or without moments of doubt and adversity.

Rising and falling, then bouncing back

In the spring of 2014, Tracie was making five-figures from her blog *every month*. Nothing, she thought, could possibly go wrong. And then, the unthinkable happened.

"I was using Amazon and making a ton of money from them alone," Tracie said. "That was until Amazon realized I was making too much and changed my commission structure. It dropped my income by 75%."

This change to Amazon's commission structure nearly cost Tracie her business. She had to let go of five employees and go three months without paying herself to cover the cost of her two remaining employees and business expenses.

While this incident temporarily cost her in mental stress and financial loss, the long-term lessons she gained were invaluable.

"[Before the Amazon commission update] I did not pursue other avenues of monetization as that was where the bulk of my income came from," she explained. "I rebuilt the biz and was smarter about the income methods I used and made sure to set it all up so that the income was distributed much more evenly from all sources."

She also realized the key to success wasn't only in her business techniques but also in her mentality as a business owner.

"It helped me realize that I had no one to blame but myself," Tracie said. "I was determined to make it work again and that drive kept me focused and allowed me to get my blogging business back on track. I rebuilt it—but the right way."

Tracie's secrets to success

Tracie's strategy and persistence ultimately paid off. She rebuilt her business with diversified revenue streams, creating a blogging business that would truly stand the test of time. Her ultimate advice? Never think you know it all.

"Be open to learning from others," she said. "It does not matter if you have been blogging for six months or six years, there is always something to learn. Being willing to make investments in my education helps me know where to focus my efforts in business growth."

When it comes to advice for bloggers who want to turn their hobby blog into a full-time online business, Tracie has these tips:

1. Have the right mindset

You have to think about your blog like a business and treat it as such. That means dedicating enough time to working on your content and marketing.

2. Invest in your business

You need to invest in education for yourself as well as in tools and people that will help your business grow. Free is attractive to new business owners on a budget, but it's not always the best answer.

3. Realize it will take time

The truth is most bloggers will not make a full-time income for a year or more. You're going to need to give it time. Don't give up just because you don't see it happening as quickly as you may like.

From hobby blogger to world class coach

After growing her first blog, Tracie longed for a career that gave her even more purpose. She loved helping people learn how to manage their money and get out of debt, but now she wanted to help people learn how to start their own successful blogging business.

Her followers had been asking her blogging and SEO advice for years, but those topics weren't a good fit for her first website. After years of putting her blood, sweat, and tears into The Penny Pinchin' Mom, Tracie knew it was time for a change. But first, she had to figure out what to do with her blog. Ultimately, she decided to sell.

Like many bloggers, it wasn't easy for Tracie to let go of her first blog, but she knew selling it was the right move for her future.

"I had to let it go so that someone else could take care of it, and I could focus on what I wanted to, which was coaching," she said.

Tracie says that bloggers who want to sell their sites in the future should invest time in building their business for purchase. This means making sure it appeals to buyers. Don't include too many personal anecdotes and keep the content more educational and informative.

After selling her site, she created TracieFobes.com, where she is able to do what she's truly passionate about—coaching.

Now, she is able to focus on helping other bloggers learn how to do what she did—build a successful blog.

"I want to see everyone achieve their financial goals and see their blogs play into that," Tracie said.

Coaching her blogging clients isn't the only thing Tracie has planned for the next few years. She's also planning some well-earned time off. Now that she's learned how to operate a blog nearly on autopilot, she can enjoy time with her family.

"I have put in a lot to build up both [blogs]," Tracie said. "I'm ready for slower paced, more relaxed days."

What Tracie's story means for you

Before starting her site, Tracie was a stay-at-home mom struggling to make ends meet. Today, she is a world-class blogging coach who built and sold a six-figure site.

Her story is unique but didn't happen because of pure luck or some miracle. Tracie devoted years of time, energy, and work into her website. She focused on her goals and invested in her education, and, most importantly, she never gave up.

Tracie is living proof that you don't have to have all the answers right away to start your own six-figure blog.

You just need to learn what to do and then do it. And keep doing it. Even if you fail the first few times, the important thing is that you keep going.

CHAPTER 9

How Susan Storm Turned a Personality Blog into a Six-Figure Purpose-Driven Company

In July 2015, Susan Storm set out to start her first blog with one goal in mind: She wanted a place to compile and organize all the information she'd learned over the years studying personality types.

At the time, Susan was a certified MBTI® (Myers-Briggs Type Indicator) practitioner as well as a freelance content marketing specialist. She'd spent years helping people understand themselves and improve their relationships through her thorough understanding of personality psychology. And she'd helped other businesses grow by creating marketing strategies and social media promotions.

While this work was fulfilling, Susan wanted a platform that would allow her to educate even more people on the transformative power of understanding and applying personality tools like the MBTI, The Big 5, and the Enneagram. And thanks to her freelance work, she already knew how to manage a blog.

So, Psychology Junkie was born.

"The purpose of [Psychology Junkie] is to help people understand themselves more clearly through the Myers-Briggs and Enneagram systems," Susan said. "I hope that readers will walk away from my blog knowing their strengths, weaknesses, and potential more fully. I also hope they will have better relationships because of their understanding of type."

Growing with purpose

Nearly one year after starting the site, Susan started to realize that it could be more than just a helpful blog about personality type. As she noticed her website traffic and revenue climbing each month, she had a light bulb moment: *This could actually become a full-time business.*

Once Susan realized that her blog could become a successful business, she immediately set out to find additional ways to monetize it. She created her first product, an e-book about stress management and the 16 personality types. She also started learning more about SEO and how to research and write articles more strategically to increase her website's traffic.

As Susan's content and SEO savvy grew, so did her business. But this progress didn't come without a few growing pains.

"Initially, I cared far too much about everyone being on the same page. When people would criticize my work, I would take it really hard," Susan said. "For a while, I tried to make my writing digestible for everyone, which essentially strained out a lot of the more useful or meaty content."

She soon realized that trying to please everyone who came to her website would be impossible. This was a difficult, but essential, lesson to learn.

"I had to learn to be okay with having some critics so that I could maintain my integrity and the accuracy of what I was writing about," Susan said. "Essentially, I had to learn to 'shake off' the mean remarks so that I could still be me and write from my perspective."

Over the next few years, Susan's blog, driven by her desire to help other people, grew into a six-figure company. Today, Psychology Junkie is one of the most popular websites about personality types, and Susan's work has been referenced by several major publications.

Getting comfortable with risk

Despite the current success of her site, there were many obstacles Susan had to climb during the first few years of starting her online business. And still today, she admits to struggling with the risks that come with being a full-time blogger.

"Google algorithms change. Pinterest algorithms change. Someone can leave a bad review of your e-book on Amazon," she said. "You have to be willing to accept a certain amount of risk and uncertainty when you decide to become a blogger."

In early 2020, Susan saw her monthly income decline by 72% month-to-month due to changes with advertising rates and the initial impact of the coronavirus pandemic.

This type of impact could easily discourage someone from pursuing a career in blogging, especially when they're supporting a large family with their blogging business, like Susan.

But Susan didn't let the revenue fluctuations derail her from her goals. In fact, she used it as motivation to work even harder.

"I've learned that I like the element of risk in a way," Susan said. "I'd rather play the game and accept the challenge and have a higher chance of winning at doing what I love than have a secure, predictable job that doesn't align with my interests."

One thing that Susan did to recover from the impact of the advertising revenue decline was focus on building her email list. She created her own personality test as an email opt-in, which drastically increased her email list, as well as her ability to market effectively to specific audiences.

Susan's tips for blogging success

Apart from getting comfortable with risk as an entrepreneur, Susan's top tips for bloggers looking to turn their blog into a full-time business are as follows:

1. *Learn how to do keyword research effectively*

Your blog content can't help anyone if they aren't able to find it. "You can write 100 articles, but if hardly anyone is looking for your content, you're going to stay in the background," Susan says.

She suggests tools, like Ubersuggest, SEM Rush, and AnswerThe-Public.com, to find relevant topics that will bring the most traffic to your site.

2. *Be consistent*

If you treat your blog like a hobby, it will stay a hobby. Treat your blog like a business, and it will become one. Work regularly—and don't make excuses.

"I started providing for my family with Psychology Junkie long before I knew it would work as successfully as it has," Susan said. "I had to really go out on a limb and treat it like a job and not a hobby (while juggling my many children), and I'm glad that I could get through the hard work, ignore the naysayers, and make it happen."

3. *Be open-minded about monetization*

Susan says that initially, she never wanted to have ads on her blog. In fact, most of the blogger resources she was following at the time said to stay away from ads because they wouldn't bring in much money. But she quickly learned that this wasn't the case.

"I made six-figures off of my blog last year, and three-quarters of my earnings were from ads," she said.

Experiment and find out what monetization methods work for you as your blog grows.

"I believe that having multiple streams of income is smart," Susan says. "Write e-books, make courses, create printable products, get affiliated with a respectable ad network. Find out what works for you."

An eye toward the future

Through her hard work and persistence, Susan was able to build a business that she is truly passionate about. She gets to share information every day about topics that help her readers. And she's not planning to stop anytime soon.

What's next for Susan and Psychology Junkie? She envisions her site becoming the top online resource for all things personality type. For Susan, this means creating a lot more content, including courses, videos, online quizzes, and books. She also wants to make Psychology Junkie more interactive for visitors as well as work on expanding her personal brand.

"While my site brings in a lot of traffic, people don't connect with the 'me' behind Psychology Junkie," Susan said. "I'm working on creating more of a personal connection with my readers."

As with any successful blog, Susan knows there will always be new opportunities to expand. And as long as she continues to produce consistent quality content for her readers, she's confident that her hard work will pay off long into the future.

"Keep your focus on the big picture and what matters to you as a person," Susan said. "I've found that if I set a goal and put everything behind it, I will find a way to get there. There may be challenges and setbacks, but you've got to have confidence in yourself and patience for the storms that show up."

CHAPTER 10

How Ben Huber and Jeff Proctor Built a Seven-Figure Blogging Enterprise

When he was 26 years old, Ben Huber had heard of the word "blog", but he wasn't sure exactly what it meant. He couldn't have guessed that this word would define his career within a few short years, but that's exactly what happened.

In his early years of entrepreneurship, Ben knew very little when it came time to learn how to start an online business. He only knew that other people had found success from online businesses, and he was enthralled with the idea that he could start, grow, and run his own company on the internet.

In February 2015, Ben partnered with a college friend, Jeff Proctor, and set out to start a website for stock analysis. The goal of the site was to help people learn how to manage their money and identify undervalued stocks to add to their holdings as part of a well-diversified portfolio.

The duo paid $100 ("That was pretty much all the money we had," Ben said.) to incorporate the business in the state of Virginia. Then they got to work.

Learning curves

After launching their first company, VTX Capital, Ben and Jeff quickly began to run into the obstacles involved in the early stages of online business. The first goal? Figuring out where to start.

"The funny part was that we didn't really have any clue what running a business entailed," Ben said. "We had no firm plan for making money other than we were going to somehow sell our advice for picking stocks."

While there were many details to iron out at this stage, the partners were motivated and eager to learn. They figured out how they could each use their unique skill sets to grow the company.

Ben had some background in website management and hosting as well as personnel management and administration experience, and Jeff had a financial planning background, having worked for an advisor for several years. While they both brought a lot to the table in terms of their own experience, they soon realized what gaps would need to be filled to make the business work.

"We realized that the content marketing side of things was infinitely harder than we could have ever imagined," Ben said. "Especially when you're bootstrapped and have no funding and no experience with media buying or marketing in general for that matter. We made great headway writing content for 12 months. But it all falls on deaf ears when you're competing with advisory services that have multi-billion dollar market caps and huge marketing departments."

At the time, their target audience consisted of mostly DIY investors who had the tenacity to learn more about buying, holding, and rebalancing their portfolios on a regular basis.

Ben and Jeff started to realize that although they were producing high-quality content for this niche market, they weren't having much luck competing with bigger sources of advisory information, such as Morningstar, Kiplinger, and Seeking Alpha.

After about 18 months of focusing on this niche, the founders decided to pivot. Both were still working full-time jobs and had been pouring their non-work hours into producing high value information. If they were going to make their company work, they agreed they needed to make a big change.

"We noticed that some of the more personal finance-oriented pieces of content on the site were gaining some organic traction—both on Pinterest and from search engines," Ben said. "In that vein, we realized that personal finance was applicable to 300 million people in the U.S. (instead of the approximately 100,000 DIY investors) and that we were having a much easier time reaching those readers than the hyper-niched investors we were more tailored to."

So, a decision was made. The business would niche out, rather than down, and focus on financial planning content that was applicable to a broader base of readers.

This move resulted in a baseline level of website traffic—and revenue—that allowed Ben and Jeff to start scaling their business.

When they had their first $700 revenue month, they started looking at what types of content were gaining social and organic traction and doubled down on what they saw was working the best.

Within four months, they exceeded $5,000 in monthly revenue, and Jeff began to make plans to leave his full-time job to focus on marketing and content creation.

Scaling up

In December 2017, Ben and Jeff made another big change. They realized the name VTX Capital didn't make sense for the new direction of their website. So, they rebranded and changed the name to something that more readers would remember and identify with—DollarSprout.

Around that same time, Ben decided to leave his corporate job and dive headfirst into making sure DollarSprout would succeed.

"Both of us quitting our jobs was like throwing gasoline on a fire. We could now put in 60+ hours a week into a formula that was very much working," Ben said. "We had our first $20,000 revenue month and had a pretty good idea of where we wanted to go next: hiring a team."

Up to this point, Ben and Jeff had been devoting every waking moment to their company. Both of the men were young, single, and living in rural Virginia at the time. Outside of their full-time jobs, DollarSprout was their sole focus.

But eventually, the duo realized that to fulfill their ultimate vision for the company, they needed to outsource some of the work.

"I'd say the first, and perhaps most stifling, mistake we made was that we operated too much in a vacuum," Ben said. "It was and always has been great to have a teammate who is as invested and interested in our business as I am. It's huge. But sometimes that lends itself to bouncing ideas solely off one another and not opening ourselves up to a world of other good ideas."

"I like to think we're pretty smart and we're half decent at learning by watching others, but there are SO many smart people out there, many of which have professional experience in so many of these fields (SEO, content curation, social media, marketing, whatever) that you'd be insane not to look up to them in one way or another."

Ben's secrets to success

Unlike some of the bloggers we interviewed, Ben says he'd always intended for his blog to become a full-time business. But even though that was the plan from Day 1, what he and Jeff lacked was a tangible plan to turn their vision into reality.

Like many first-time business owners, the team faced several challenges, but after 18 months of hard work and persistence, they finally started to see the fruits of their labor.

Today, DollarSprout has more than 12 million readers, five full-time employees, and numerous contractors and brings in over seven-figures annually. But one thing Ben stresses is that their success didn't happen overnight, and many lessons were learned along the way.

Here are Ben's top secrets to success for bloggers:

1. Be prepared to commit

"Full-time online business is a commitment, especially if you're currently in a 9 to 5," Ben said. "The reality is that there is going to be some level of commitment to working during most of your available free time."

For many bloggers, this isn't a problem. They genuinely enjoy online business and all the activities it entails.

But the more you have going on in your life, the harder it can be to commit the long hours required to grow your blog. This is why it's imperative to not only commit to devoting time to work but also time to learn how to work smarter, not harder.

"In such a competitive landscape, even A+ content is hard to get out there, and so when you immerse yourself in the digital marketing environment and commit to learning an array of skill sets, over time, you'll start to acquire a well-rounded acumen for promoting your content," Ben said. "But again, all of this revolves around time spent creating content and learning."

2. Find what works, then go all-in

As you grow as a blogger, you'll begin to develop a well-rounded marketing skill set. However, it's often easier to grow your audience and revenue through a single medium. Thus, Ben suggests learning early on where your audience is most active and going all-in on learning that platform.

"TikTok, Snapchat, YouTube, Google, Pinterest, whatever it be, dominate a particular platform before you try to be in eight places at once," Ben said.

He advises bloggers to become a pro at a few things first rather than putting the bare minimum effort into many things just to maintain a presence.

"Double down on what's working for you and commit to mastering the ins and outs of that particular platform," Ben said. "Then once you've built an audience, leverage the success you're having there to diversify into other platforms. That way, your eggs aren't all in one basket if a particular platform makes a cataclysmic change."

3. *Ride your highs while you're high but know that there will also be lows*

Entrepreneurship seems glamorous, but it's a lot of work. And the ups and downs that come with growing a blogging business can result in highs and lows. Ben suggests that bloggers take advantage of the high moments but also go easy on themselves when they're not feeling so great.

"Burnout is real, and there will be many, many times where you find yourself struggling to focus on the task at hand," Ben said. "When you're in the zone, try to stay there as long as you can and minimize distractions. This can happen on a minute-by-minute basis, or there can be weeks on end where you're really motivated and enjoying a particular task. You're hyper-efficient during those times so double down when you find you're in the zone."

"The same can be said about when you're not feeling it," he continued. "It's a dangerous place to be, and you can waste dozens of hours per week when you're distracted by a laundry list of things you could potentially be doing around the house."

On the days when you feel frequently distracted or low energy, Ben suggests cutting yourself some slack.

"Get out, go take a break, and come back and try again later," he said.

4. Find a team that you trust

One of the most essential lessons that Ben learned was the importance of finding people who are willing to help you succeed.

In fact, he says, the larger his blogging business became, the harder it was to find people he could genuinely trust. So if you find competent and trustworthy people early on, make sure to maintain the relationships.

"My advice would be to find a core group of people that you know and trust and lean on them to get the majority of your advice," Ben said. "There's so much noise and so many people saying different things that it's hard to filter out what matters."

Unless you are willing to spend a lot of money, Ben says, after a certain point there are fewer people who want to work with you to grow your site because they may see you as competition.

"Don't get me wrong, there are plenty of selfless people willing to help at all stages," Ben said. "But it's often very hard for people to discern who is trying to make money off them, and who does exactly that, but provides legitimate value."

As you scale, Ben says to find generalists who have successfully scaled a blog and soak up as much as you can from them. If you're looking for specialized knowledge, such as advanced Facebook ads or affiliate management software implementation, look to solicit help from single field gurus who know that subject intimately.

5. *Never stop learning*

As essential as it is to find people you can trust to help you grow your blog, know that your blog's success will still depend on your own commitment to continually learn and improve.

"While there are certainly very helpful people out there, there isn't always going to be someone there to hold your hand and help you along when you're stuck or confused," Ben said. "It's going to take a commitment to a LOT of learning, trial and error, Googling, and fixing things yourself when they inevitably break."

Depending on your own background and experience, certain facets of blog ownership can be more challenging than others. Sometimes, Ben explains, it just takes sucking it up and getting your hands dirty until you figure some of the more difficult things out.

"It's notably frustrating when you're learning how to design and tinker with your blog since the technical side is often a headache if you don't have a web developer background, but it doesn't stop once you finally get your blog looking the way you want it to," he said. "Different complexities arise. Great, now you've got your blog setup, traffic, and maybe a little income, but then the challenge becomes how in the world do you best put that income to use to scale/grow your blog?"

This is where learning opportunities, such as courses, masterminds, and mentorships, can be extremely beneficial.

"Find a way to rub shoulders or work with people that are smarter than you. It's the best way to grow and learn more about the field we work in," Ben said. "If you're complacent, think you know it all, or find something that works but don't iterate, you're 100% going to fall behind the curve."

CHAPTER 11

Going Beyond Your Blog

Launching a successful blogging business is no easy feat. It takes hard work, determination, grit, and, most importantly, persistence. However, if you stick with it and follow the advice we've shared within the pages of this book, your hard work will pay off.

It's true. You can become very rich and successful from blogging alone. However, many blogging entrepreneurs ultimately end up wanting to diversify their income streams even further, or they want to grow their brand beyond the scope of their blog.

There are several ways to promote your brand and increase authority as an expert in your niche outside of your blog. Some of the most popular tactics include:

● Book publishing

- Public speaking

- Coaching and consulting

Book publishing

If you've already built a successful blog, self-publishing is an excellent way to expand your brand presence and build on your authority. Some of the most successful bloggers work with publishing houses and take the traditional publishing route. However, these days it's easier than ever for anyone with the desire to create and access to the internet to publish a book.

What's more—you don't need to be an expert in publishing or even marketing to create, distribute, and sell your book. Platforms, like Amazon's Kindle Direct Publishing (KDP), walk you through the necessary steps to self-publish and even provide marketing support in some cases.

The first step in book publishing is deciding what you want to write a book about. When determining your book topic, there are a few things you need to consider:

- **Is the topic relevant to your niche, and does it solve a problem?** You want your existing readers and followers to buy your book, so make sure that it's a topic that solves a common problem they face. Look at some of your most popular blog posts to get a better idea of what your readers are most interested in.

- **Is the topic evergreen?** Evergreen content continues to stay fresh and relevant over time. If your blog is seasonal (if you blog solely about summer vacation destinations, for example), then that would be an exception. You may also want to publish something to promote around a holiday or season if there is a large interest in that from your audience. However, evergreen content will ensure that sales stay consistent over time. You can use tools, like Google Trends, to determine seasonality.

- **Is there high demand but low competition for your topic?** The most successful books will be in categories where there is high demand but low competition. You can conduct keyword research on your topic and look at the keyword difficulty and search volume to determine overall demand and competition for a given word or phrase.

After you decide on your topic, you'll need to decide how to create your book. Will you write it from scratch? You likely already have a few blog posts that can be compiled into content for your book. If you're not up for writing the whole thing yourself, you could also hire a freelance ghostwriter to help with the writing process.

The next step is the book design. Unless you're an expert designer, you'll need to outsource this step. Your cover design is the first impression people will get of your book, so you'll want to make sure it's professional, appealing, and reflective of your brand. You will likely also need to have a designer format the book for both print and digital distribution.

Once you have a complete book, it's time to publish! You can publish your book on your own blog, sell it on third-party websites, such as Amazon, or a mix for maximum distribution. Just keep in mind that certain resellers have guidelines that make it so that you can only sell on their site and nowhere else, so make sure you read the fine print if you choose to sell with a third-party.

When your book is ready to launch, share it with your email list, social media followers, and friends and family. Then sit back and watch as the income flows in. You're an author!

Public speaking

Public speaking isn't for every blogger, but if you're energized by crowds and amplifying your message in a different way, it could be the right path for you.

Like with publishing a book, speaking is another way to repurpose your existing blog content. You can turn a top blog post into a speech for a live or virtual event. Another more modern way to explore public speaking is by sharing your story on podcasts or social media interviews.

These mediums aren't simply a fantastic way to share your message with a larger audience of potential readers and followers, but you can also use them to promote new products or services.

So, where do you start? The best way to get your foot in the door when it comes to public speaking is good old-fashioned networking.

Although in the age of blogging and social media, networking doesn't quite look the way it used to.

Most connections these days are made by reaching out and engaging with other influencers and thought leaders in your niche. If you have a direct request and something valuable to offer their audience, that's great. But it never hurts to make a connection early on. You may not have anything specific to offer now, but if you make a connection early, it will be less awkward when you reach out again down the road.

For many live and virtual events, you can find applications to speak on the event website. But it never hurts to find out who is planning the event and reach out directly as well. Make it clear that you're interested in speaking and explain why your information is so valuable. The more that you can prove you are an authority in a topic, the better chance you have at being selected to speak. So don't be shy!

Coaching and consulting

Another method you can use to promote your brand and increase authority as an expert in your niche is offering coaching and/or consulting services. If you're looking for a purely passive income, this method may not be for you. However, if you have a skill or expertise that you're passionate about, consider turning it into a service offering.

For example, maybe you have a quick-and-easy way to conduct SEO audits for your blog. It may take you less than 30 minutes to conduct an audit. But the end result is extremely valuable to bloggers new to SEO. You can charge a premium rate for your auditing service without sacrificing a large amount of your time unless you want to, of course.

If you're a people-person, you may enjoy one-on-one or group coaching sessions. Remember Tracie's story (Chapter 8)? Tracie realized that what she was most passionate about is coaching other bloggers, so she pivoted and focused her entire business on doing just that.

You may begin to realize through blogging that your passion lies more in performing a specific service, book publishing, public speaking, or something totally different! Don't be afraid to let what pulls on your heartstrings guide you. Remember, this is only the beginning of your journey. Where you go next is up to you!

A Final Note

By now, we hope you feel prepared to launch your blog from a side hustle to a six-figure business. And while we have mostly focused on earning six-digits in this book, that is by no means the limit to earning potential when it comes to blogging.

Did you know that The Huffington Post, one of the most popular blogs of all time, earns $40 million dollars per month? Most bloggers don't have the resources that HuffPo has. However, there are many blogging legends that got started just like you.

These entrepreneurs started blogging while working a full-time job or raising a family. They started with only a few spare dollars in their pockets. They sacrificed late nights and time with friends to make things work. And now, some of these bloggers are earning more than $100,000 per month!

You, too, can build a successful blogging business. But you have to be open and willing to invest in yourself—invest your time, your money, your energy—and, most importantly, don't give up. There will inevitably be ups and downs along your journey. You will succeed. You will fail.

But you're not alone on this path. There are so many others who are on the same journey. Connect with like-minded people. Learn from them, just like you've learned from the blogging heroes we featured in this book. Apply the lessons you've learned here and start creating the life you want to live.

Are you ready?

One More Thing!

We hope you enjoyed reading this book as much as Megan and I enjoyed writing it. If you'd like to hear more, head over to EinsteinBlogging.com where you can join our email list to stay up-to-date on blogging and business trends, advice for bloggers, and more.

Additionally, we offer content creation, marketing, and book publishing services for bloggers just like you. You can connect with me personally anytime on Instagram or Twitter (@forrestpwebber), and you can find Megan on Instagram and Twitter, too (@meganmmalone).

Finally, if you liked this book, please let me know by leaving a review or reaching out to me directly at EinsteinBlogging.com. Looking forward to hearing from you!

— *Forrest*

www.ingramcontent.com/pod-product-compliance
Lightning Source LLC
LaVergne TN
LVHW051343050326
832903LV00031B/3709